Judicial Reorganization

Judicial Reorganization

The Politics of Reform in the Federal Bankruptcy Court

Carroll Seron
The University of Texas at Dallas

Lexington Books
D.C. Heath and Company
Lexington, Massachusetts
Toronto

Library of Congress Cataloging in Publication Data

Seron, Carroll.
    Judicial reorganization.

    Bibliography: p.
    Includes index.
    1. Bankruptcy—United States. I. Title.
KF1527.S4   346'.73'078   77–234
ISBN 0–669–01435–4

Published simultaneously in Canada

Printed in the United States of America

International Standard Book Number: 0–669–01435–4

Library of Congress Catalog Card Number: 77–234

*For My Mother and Father,
Andrea, and Donna*

Contents

List of Figures and Tables

Acknowledgments

This book is part of a larger study of the United States Federal Courts. It is to Wolf Heydebrand, the director of this project, that I owe my greatest intellectual debt. At every stage of this study, he offered constructive criticism, along with sincere encouragement, which then provided a point of departure for the development of my own work. I am also grateful to Herbert Menzel for his unusual care in reading earlier drafts of this study. Edwin Shur's insightful suggestions clarified many points. I am especially grateful for the friendships that evolved in working on this study.

Many other friends and colleagues gave their support; my gratitude to them is enormous. Louanne Kennedy patiently endured long hours of conversation, read many drafts, and provided encouragement during some difficult hours of writing. Eleanor Westney and Betty Farrell read revised chapters, often at a moment's notice, and offered important points of clarification. And Donna Healey constantly reminded me that political issues must always be central to one's work.

Financial assistance creates the critical atmosphere for writing—time, space, and a comfortable place to work. I was fortunate to have all three. I received assistance for the first phase of this project from the Russell Sage Foundation; I am particularly grateful to Arnold Shore of the Russell Sage Foundation for his friendly reassurance. I received assistance for the final phase of this project through a NIMH Grant (5-T01 NH 13124-05) to Yale University for a Postdoctoral Fellowship in Deviance, Social Control, and the Sociology of Law. I would like to thank Albert Reiss and Stanton Wheeler for this unique opportunity. Of course, whatever errors remain in the study are my own responsibility.

Evridiki Savidis, Joan Cianciolo, Florence Cohen, Pamela Colesworthy, and Rotha Lane typed various parts of this manuscript. I fondly thank them for all their efforts.

Finally, my greatest personal debt is to Frank Sayre for patience, understanding, and humor without which this book would have been far more difficult to complete.

1 The Structure of the Bankruptcy Court

Myriad questions surround any discussion about the role of the federal court in the late twentieth century. These questions seek to discover whether the court is an effective "check" upon the executive and legislative branches, whether the court articulates state policy, or, perhaps whether the federal court is an antiquated organization from a bygone era (Jacob 1965; Peltason 1955; Richardson and Vines 1970). The last of these questions is the focus of this research: the analysis of judicial reform. Judicial reform has traditionally referred to avenues for improving the administrative efficiency of courts (Gallas et al. 1971). This relatively narrow concern with court efficiency, however, anticipates the issue of organizational change in the courts, or the larger problem of rationalizing and modernizing judicial processes.

Recent developments within the United States Bankruptcy Court provide a unique opportunity to study the process of court reform as a process of potential rationalization or organizational change. The bankruptcy court, a part of the United States District Court system, is charged with the adjudication of bankruptcy cases. It is a right of American citizens to declare themselves bankrupt and to liquidate most debts if they can show that present financial circumstances will not permit payment without severe hardship. Since bankruptcy derives from federal statutes, all American citizens (i.e., consumers and corporations) who use this procedure fall within federal jurisdiction. In the post-World War II period, the significant increase in bankruptcy cases has strained the present organizational structure of the court and its relationship to the district court. Reform proposals have been under consideration by committees in the House and the Senate that would fundamentally alter the court's organization.[1]

One proposal suggests that bankruptcy cases be removed from the auspices of the judicial branch and be placed in the executive. Initially, bankruptcy cases would be treated as tasks to be processed by an administrative agency, rather than as adversarial procedures. It also proposes the establishment of a specialized court that would handle those cases in which a controversy between debtor and creditor arose. The model of this reform implies a structure analogous to the relationship between the Internal Revenue Service and the tax court. The underlying assumption of this proposal is that most bankruptcy procedures are relatively straightforward and can be more effectively and rationally handled by an administrative agency than by a court of law. This proposal, then, suggests a basically *bureaucratic alternative* for court reform.

The second proposal seeks to remove the bankruptcy court from the auspices of the district court and to establish a separate and distinct bankruptcy court. The argument of this proposal is that bankruptcy as a legal procedure has come of age and that the complexity of the cases demands an autonomous court structure. This proposal, by contrast, suggests a *professionalized alternative* for court reform.

While both proposals also suggest various changes in the specific chapters of the Bankruptcy Code, an overriding difference is to be found in how and where legal procedures will be executed. A major point of contention is over which type of organizational structure will be most effective for handling the work of this court. Should steps be taken to make this court an administrative agency or an autonomous judicial organization? In fact, the proposals reflect antithetical solutions.

An important political question is central to this research. The analysis of court reform may demonstrate the limits of a traditional adversarial organization, that is, a collegial, professional court of law. As it faces reform, the court epitomizes a legal institution caught between the libertarian tradition of adjudication (i.e., due process and the rule of law) and the organizational reality of heavy demand. The possible removal of bankruptcy procedures from the judiciary challenges the organizational foundation of this branch.

The establishment of an administrative agency to process bankruptcy cases may temporarily solve the immediate problem of delay and demand; however, to the extent that this solution undermines access to an adjudicatory setting and becomes an increasingly common model for other courts, both state and federal, the political rights which that system seeks to guarantee are in jeopardy. While the actual reform of the court remains a political question that has not been resolved, it nevertheless reflects a larger trend in our entire court system. The implications drawn from this study move beyond the confines of the bankruptcy court.

The challenge to these due process rights derives from the organizational structure that may be implemented to process legal questions. In fact, this trend is already apparent: the "Roosevelt revolution" secured a permanent place for administrative law, and with it the rise of "sociological law" (Auerbach 1976; Lowi 1969; Davis 1975; Schubert 1960). Moreover, this historical development has also introduced to the legal community the modern, rational organizational setting—an organizational structure that is fundamentally different from collegial courts of law. In essence, the reform of the court may further support a social structure that must increasingly rely upon rational bureaucratic control as contrasted with more collegial organizational structures.

The reform proposals for the bankruptcy court symbolize contradictory strategies for the coordination and execution of legal questions. The supporters of the bureaucratic alternative—a common panacea of social reformers—must contend with conservative objections to their strategy. They must contend with the entrenched and established judiciary; rationalization (formal rules, hierarchical structure, formal office, etc.) is seen to challenge the position and authority of the traditional legal community (Auerbach 1976). "The struggle over court reform can thus be taken as a strategic research site where the organizational contradictions within the judiciary can be studied, and where the forces of rationalization confront the more and more conscious resistance of the judiciary itself" (Heydebrand 1977a, p. 97).

On the other hand, it can be argued that the bureaucratization of legal procedure will exacerbate *inequality of access* to the judicial system. Bankruptcy affects consumers and corporations; the supporters of the bureaucratic alternative propose that all cases be filed with an agency and only proceed to a courtroom, adversarial setting if a controversy between parties develops. Obviously, controversies are more common or usual in corporate cases where the financial stakes are greater. Insofar as the bureaucratic alternative provides a screening device to filter out "simpler" (i.e., consumer) cases, it supports a more "effective" setting for corporate-type cases. So long, however, as the right to review is incorporated into a reform proposal, that strategy remains within the law (Davis 1975). That is, consumer bankrupts, under the bureaucratic alternative, will still technically have the right to judicial review, to due process of the law. The question is, how accessible is that review process? Clearly there is a stratification implied in the bureaucratic alternative for court reform. This possible outcome of court reform supports Mannheim's argument that "the fundamental tendency of all bureaucratic thought is to turn all problems of politics into problems of administration" (1936, p. 118). The bureaucratic outcome of court reform, then, may actually be a conservative response to the liberal demand for change and in the final analysis further undermine the Constitutional right to due process of the law.

An Overview of the Bankruptcy Court

To return to an earlier point, both consumer and corporate bankruptcies fall within federal jurisdiction. Such cases were formerly heard by federal court judges as part of their larger civil and criminal responsibilities. However, as the number of bankruptcy cases grew and their distinct quality became increasingly clear, deputy judges, or what were later referred to as referees, were authorized to hear bankruptcy cases (Parness 1973). In 1938 the deputy judge review process was formalized with a reform of bankruptcy procedures: as of that date, referees in bankruptcy were given authority to grant discharges of debt to an individual or corporation, an authority formerly reserved for federal district court judges.

Therefore in 1938, reform of the district court established an important precedent by granting judicial decision-making responsibility to personnel other than judges. Two aspects of this reform distinguish the bankruptcy court from the larger district court. First, referees in bankruptcy are appointed by the judges of a district and work under the auspices of that district for a period of six years; district judges are appointed by the president and serve for the duration of their lives. Second, the determinations made by referees are subject to review by the district court; district court judges are subject to review by the appeals court of the circuit.

While selection of the referees and review of their decisions by the district demarcate a separate organization, these processes simultaneously place that organization under the control and supervision of the district court. District court judges speak for a court, but the decision of referees may be overturned in the very court in which they reside. In other words, referees serve the district court by making decisions on either fact or law, but they cannot speak for the court. The referee is a *para-judge*; the structure of this court is a *para-judicial* organization.

The organizational rationale for this parajudicial court within the federal court system has been that bankruptcy law defines a specialized knowledge base.[2] Bankruptcy law can be analytically divided into two basic areas: consumer or individual bankruptcy, and corporate or business bankruptcy. Within each of these analytic categories there are, again, two distinct legal options: straight bankruptcy, or plans of rearrangment and reorganization (see figure 1–1). In straight bankruptcy, the individual or corporation uses the auspices of the court to permit nonpayments (or liquidation) of debts; the court grants a discharge of payment of debts or orders the sale of assets to pay part or all of the debts involved. In plans of rearrangement or reorganization, the respective chapters of the Bankruptcy Code establish slightly different legal procedures for consumer and corporate cases. In general, however, the bankrupt party seeks to establish a plan of payment of debts over a designated period of time under the auspices of the court. This process, in turn, permits the individual or the corporation to become solvent again and recover as a viable economic actor. There are two alternatives for the initiation of bankruptcy proceedings: voluntary bankruptcy, a process in which the party claiming bankruptcy may enter the court to make such a filing, or involuntary bankruptcy, a process in which creditors owed money by individuals or corporations may enter the court and demand that the parties meet their obligations.

The specialized nature of bankruptcy law has also supported the development of a circumscribed group of lawyers, trustees, and referees whose primary work is in this area of law (Kennedy 1975). While the bankruptcy court is formally embedded in the federal district court, it can nevertheless be examined as an autonomous organization with a distinct organizational environment, set of tasks, personnel, resources, and dispositions.

Each of these categories represents a cluster of theoretical issues and empirical variables that describes the bankruptcy court. That is, the *environmental*

	STRAIGHT BANKRUPTCY	PLANS OF REARRANGEMENT
INDIVIDUAL/CONSUMER CASES	Chapters I–VIII	Chapter XIII
BUSINESS/CORPORATE CASES	Chapters I–VIII	Chapter X, XI

Figure 1-1. Diagram of the Tasks of the Court by Chapter of
the Bankruptcy Code

profile—the U.S. Federal District—is, in part, the nexus of specific economic, social, and demographic patterns that have affected the caseload and casemix, i.e., *task structure,* of this court on the one hand and the development of a specialized bankruptcy bar, i.e., *organizational matrix* (Kennedy and Seron 1975) on the other. In turn, the caseload and casemix along with the legal community, i.e., *task environment,* have affected the development and allocation of judicial and nonjudicial personnel and resources, i.e., *size,* to this court. Finally, those who work in this court are responsible for the terminations and dispositions, i.e., *effectiveness,* of the bankruptcy court. Figure 1-2 schematically describes this court and the causal relationship between these clusters of variables. As the figure indicates, the economic and demographic indicators of the court's environment are independent variables. The task structure, organizational matrix, and size are intervening variables, and effectiveness is the dependent variable.

Each of these "quantitative" variables is open for political debate during the process of court reform. That is, the relationship among organizational factors is the historical outcome of economic, social, and demographic forces as well as active, practical political debate. The chapters that follow seek to

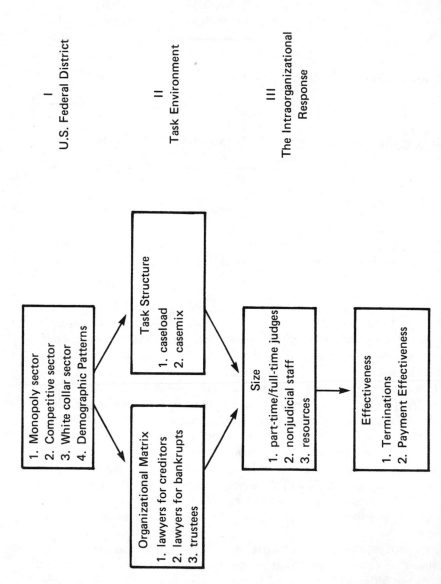

Figure 1-2. Causal Schema of Analysis of Organizational Formation of Bankruptcy Court

show the theoretical and empirical relationship among these factors in the case of the formation and transformation of the bankruptcy court.

Chapter 2, then, is a review and overview of issues in organizational theory and methodology that provides an anchor point for this study. Chapter 3 examines the historical relationship between the court's environment and task structure, and the political debate that this issue raises in the process of reform. Chapter 4 examines the historical relationship between the court's environment and the development of a cohesive and strong legal community, and the debate over its future connection to this court in the process of reform. Chapter 5 focuses on the court's use of judicial and nonjudicial personnel and resources, and the political issues that these central factors raise in the process of reform. Finally, Chapter 6 examines the question of the court's organizational and political effectiveness: who has historically benefited from this court? And, by extension, who benefits in the process of reform (Blau and Scott 1962)? This court has become a more important forum within American law, but has it maintained its stated goal of providing an "orderly" and judicious framework for its bankrupts, its clients? Or, has this court created an effective forum for supporting a matrix of professionals at the cost of its clients?

One other point is in order and is, perhaps, a justification for the structure of the chapters that follow. Some may argue that the presentation of findings is cumbersome, if not tedious. Recognizing this problem, I have attempted to present this material in as interesting a manner as possible; but I have not sacrificed many of the details of this debate. This decision was deliberate. For it is only by examining the sometimes subtle differences among various groups on a particular facet of a larger debate that we can hope to unravel the complexities of social reform. Hence, the emphasis in this study is on the process, not the effects, of reform in one small area, the bankruptcy court. But the story of this process is, I think, worth telling both for what it reveals about the possible future of our legal institutions as well as for what it suggests about how marginal groups of all kinds might more effectively partake in public debates.

In one sense, the work pursued here is exploratory. While research in organizations is an ever-expanding area, the conceptual framework developed (see chapter 2) and the study of a court from a comparative organizational perspective both represent new avenues. Therefore, this research poses a new direction for organizational analysis in general, and courts in particular, rather than a retesting of a question that has been explored by others. Most importantly, this study demands that we consider the contradictory implications of judicial reform: in an attempt to make the organization of the court more effective and efficient, reform may further undermine the right to exercise the due process cornerstone of our legal system.

Notes

1. Hearings are being held by the Subcommittee on Judicial Machinery of the Committee on the Judiciary in the Senate, and the Subcommittee of the Committee on the Judiciary in the House of Representatives.

2. As an alternative to the parajudicial court organization based on specialized knowledge, one might examine the Popular Tribunals of Cuba, the Comradely Court of Russia, and the People's Court of China (see Berman 1960).

2

The Structural Constraints of Court Reform

Common to contemporary developments in organizational models has been a continuing dialogue with the Weberian perspective. Beginning with the early case studies of Gouldner (1954) and Blau (1955) researchers have continued to examine the Weberian model and have continued also to suggest significant modifications in its content. In fact, even as organizational research was moved into the comparative realm, where the unit of analysis is the organization itself, the dialogue with Weber has continued.

The Weberian Challenge

Although contemporary analysts of organizations often use Weber's work as a springboard, such researchers frequently assume that the criteria of bureaucratic organization are given; hence, it is assumed that there is no need to consider the more macropolitical implications of definitions that are both contained within Weber's work itself and provide critical frameworks for the study of organizational formations.

Weber's analysis of bureaucracy, a component of his political sociology, evolves from his study of domination.[1] For Weber, the state, or governmental processes, can be examined as independent entities with independent roles: "Every type of domination depends [for control] upon an administrative apparatus under a chief or ruling body . . ." (Bendix 1962, p. 482).

For Weber, the social relations of domination are not adequately explained by the relations of socioeconomic class; rather, they are explained by political forms of domination and by the composition of the state. In this regard, Weber is less concerned with the origins of capitalism, but rather with the processes of thought (or legitimacy) and the apparatuses of control (or bureaucracy) that are manifest in societies.[2] In the occidental modern world, social processes are epitomized by the term *rationalization*: "Rationalization and disenchantment result in the fragmentation of the knower into a one-sided specialist, and the fragmentation of knowledge into separate, partial systems constituted according to one-sided viewpoints" (Roth 1971, p. 26). Therefore, it would seem, the critical relations to analyze are the processes by which organizations change and possibly become more rational.

The most compelling part of Weber's analysis of bureaucracy is his understanding and examination of the coordinative aspects of bureaucracy itself—what

9

makes bureaucracy precise, speedy, and technically superior. A court, for example, is a collegial organization[3] and yet a court, like all modern organizations, to survive as a viable structure must, given the Weberian position, come to mirror a rationalized administration. The technical superiority of bureaucratization lies in the internal characteristics of the bureaucratic structure and, for Weber, has little to do with the larger social contradictions of class relations or political equality and economic inequality.[4]

Contemporary bureaucratic organization is rationalized domination legitimated by belief in enacted rules and impersonal order. The cornerstone of bureaucracy is the office, through which the importance of position comes to supersede the importance of the person: "the official serves *not* the ruler who appoints him in a personal manner, but the *impersonal* demands of his office" (Cohen 1972, p. 67).[5]

Selection to office demands competence in a limited sphere of work. The "pervasive element" that links officials to their defined sphere of work within a hierarchical structure is "the existence of a system of control based upon rational rules, rules which try to regulate the whole organizational structure and process on the basis of technical knowledge and the aim of maximum efficiency" (Mouzelis 1972, p. 39).

Technical knowledge in concert with official appointment epitomizes rational bureaucratic administration. Or, as Weber puts it,

Bureaucratic administration means fundamentally domination through knowledge. This is the feature which makes it specifically rational. This consists, on the one hand, in technical knowledge which, by itself, is sufficient to ensure it a position of extraordinary power. But in addition to this, bureaucratic organizations, or the holders of power who make use of them, have the tendency to increase their power still further by the knowledge growing out of experience in the service. For they acquire through the conduct of office a special knowledge of facts and have available a store of documentary material peculiar to themselves. (Weber 1968, p. 225)

Stammler (1971) points out that the study of organizations, understood from a Weberian perspective, should take rationalization, or the process by which an organization moves in the direction of hierarchical, rule-bound, formal procedures, as the central criteria for analysis. This process should be examined as a "relative" one, that is by considering the place of rational procedure in the life of the larger organizational structure. The Weberian challenge is not simply to analyze organizations as bureaucratic, traditional, or charismatic, but rather to examine the processes by which organizations become rationally controlled.

The focus for investigation is, therefore, the "power struggle" involved in the transition to rational domination.[6] This transitional process begins at the "apex" of the bureaucratic structure. The apex of organizational formations, however, is nonbureaucratic; it is a political matrix that, in fact, controls the division of labor (Stinchcombe 1965).

The Weberian perspective places emphasis upon the internal paradoxes of organizations; it thus provides a convenient starting point to formulate a perspective on organizational formation and transformation. However, it is also necessary to consider how one might examine social, political, and economic dynamics that are external to the development of the particular organization under study. Comparative organizational theory and analysis provide clues to such an explanation. The emphasis in comparative analysis has been on the examination of organizational relationships (for example, among size, professionalization, span of control, etc.) regardless of the specific type of organizations in which these relationships appear. (See, for example, Blau 1968, 1970; Blau, Heydebrand, and Stauffer 1966; Heydebrand 1973a, 1973b; Meyer 1972a, 1972b, 1975.) On the one hand, this development reflects a refinement of the Weberian perspective insofar as the model of legal-rational bureaucracy exists in other, nongovernmental settings, particularly business firms. On the other hand, however the comparative analytic approach almost uniformly ignores the more macropolitical questions central to the Weberian perspective. Consequently, traditional organizational research has not yet addressed the following types of questions: what is the significance for the larger society of the possible rationalization of a particular type of organization? What causes a particular type of organization to become more rational? Is rationalization the only direction for the transformation of an organization?

The Weberian Echo: Contemporary Developments in Organizational Theory

Comparative organizational analysis has moved in two significant but different directions, those of *interorganizational analysis* and *longitudinal analysis*. Both movements reflect an attempt to more adequately address two crucial issues: the relationship of the focal organization to its larger social milieu, and the effects of changing intraorganizational patterns upon the focal organization under examination.

Interorganizational analysis, which emphasizes examination of organizational relationships, has gone through a number of developmental phases. Preliminary work relied upon ad hoc typologies that provided frameworks for examining the "field" surrounding a focal organization (Emery and Trist 1965; Marrat 1971; Terreberry 1968).

The general hypothesis in interorganizational work has been that intraorganizational mechanisms cannot be assessed without reference to the larger environment of an organization. Thus the following issues must be considered. First is the political "struggles" between organizations; this issue re-examines the Weberian assumptions concerning rationalization as an inevitable direction of social change.[7] Second is the "ecological" examination of the organization in its environmental setting; this issue modifies the rigid boundary that has been drawn in much organizational analysis between the organization itself and its surrounding social milieu.[8] Third is the specification of organizational analysis as a forum for the creation of class relations as well as for the maintenance of class relations; this issue considers the political question of "effective" control of rationalization by adding the important second question—effective control for whom?[9]

Interorganizational analysis has to date reflected an emphasis upon synchronic analysis. (But see Meyer 1975.) Although the issues posed above are logical outgrowths of this perspective, they do not, in fact, accurately reflect the work in organizational analysis that has been completed to date. The synthesis of the above questions implies a perspective of change that is just now beginning to be elaborated in the area of longitudinal analysis of organizations. However, analysis of process in and of itself is not the analysis of process in a *historical* context. Considerations of historical specificity go beyond purely diachronic considerations.

Most longitudinal analyses have relied upon purely ad hoc time points of comparison. It is necessary, then, to reconsider the assumptions of existing longitudinal analysis and to incorporate significant points in time as benchmarks for the focal organization under examination. The researcher must be guided by historical inquiry into the qualitative developments of a particular organizational problem. These considerations must focus on the organization under examination in particular, but consideration should also be given to changing economic, demographic, and ecological factors as well. In other words, even the quite obvious organizational question of growth and decline is in part related to the environmental factors relevant to the organization under examination.[10] To date, longitudinal analysis has not given adequate consideration to this problem.

Interorganizational and longitudinal analysis have basically developed without reference to each other. Interorganizational analysis has moved beyond the boundaries of the organization and has incorporated the analysis of "linkages" (for example, domain, risk, interaction, dependence, etc.) and other demographic considerations in order to understand the internal processes of that organization and in order to establish that organization's place in the larger community. However, most studies have relied upon a synchronic perspective. Longitudinal analysis, on the other hand, has moved beyond synchronic analysis but has failed to consider interorganizational relations. In other words, in interorganizational analysis a change dimension has been sacrificed for ecological considerations, whereas in longitudinal analysis ecological considerations have been sacrificed for a change dimension.

Interorganizational analysis has demonstrated that organizations do not exist in a vacuum, without contacts with the society surrounding the organization under study. Longitudinal analysis has demonstrated that the examination of organizations over time challenges some previous assumptions concerning the coordination of activities to produce an organization's "goal," be it teaching students or curing patients (Meyer 1972b). Both perspectives share, however, with Weber's work an underlying assumption that organizations change in a unilinear direction. In the case of interorganizational research this is apparent in the widespread assumption that the organization in its environmental setting (regardless of how environment is operationalized) need be examined at only one point in time, in fact at any point in time. In the case of longitudinal research this is apparent in the assumption that inquiry into the determination of time points selected for study is by and large not important. Organizations are assumed to be ahistorical social structures.

The ahistorical foundation of these perspectives is epitomized in the fusion of process and outcome into a single analytic construct. Though Weber's construct of rational bureaucracy is examined as the historical outcome of economic, social, and political forces particular to western history, rational bureaucracy, (in this case the German civil service) examined in its contemporary context, is treated as a static phenomenon.

An organization is a formally established structure designed to accomplish a given set of tasks. This resultant organization is a conscious creation by human beings. The establishment of a formal structure to accomplish a given task is a *historical* outcome, a historical product. If organizations are historical outcomes, then they are "more or less incomplete, more or less imperfect historical objectifications of conscious, practical activity" (Heydebrand 1977a, p. 85). Organizations contain potentially *contradictory* dynamics that can be understood only if seen in a historical context. If we return to Weber's construct of rational bureaucracy and reconsider his "criteria" for such organization as "more or less incomplete," rather than as finite categories, it becomes apparent that the introduction of written rules, as one example, may, in the work setting of a court or a hospital, come into conflict with the professional autonomy of judges or doctors. The historical introduction of written (that is, bureaucratic) rules that define the work setting within a hospital or a court may challenge the historically older structure of professional (that is, craft) autonomy and control. However, this potential contradiction between rule structures must be seen as historically possible, not as historically inevitable. Thus, the establishment of the bankruptcy court in 1938 as an organization, separate and distinct from the district court, is the political manifestation of economic and social forces: it is one possible organizational outcome of a judicial system—the establishment of an autonomous and specialized court to adjudicate bankruptcy cases.

What an organization does and how an organization works are, therefore, processes of ongoing organizational activity. However, these processes of organizational activity are constrained by resources (i.e., technologies) that are limited by the historical time of establishment and circumscribe the possibility of change for that organization. Change within the organization is constrained by that organization's history, the process of its formation. For example, the formation of the bankruptcy court as established in 1938 both permits the addition of judicial and nonjudicial personnel as a solution to backlog and defines the domain of the court as the jurisdiction of the United States Federal District. The resultant bankruptcy cases within that jurisdiction are the responsibility of the court. Thus, organizational activity within the bankruptcy court is constrained by both the possibility of adding judicial and nonjudicial personnel and the bankruptcies within the United States Federal District. This, in part, circumscribes the possibility of change within the bankruptcy court as it presently exists.

The question then arises: can these processes of ongoing organizational activity give rise to a qualitative change of an organization's structure? Insofar as an organization is a consciously created structure, that structure may be consciously transformed. Again, the possibility of such change is a historically specific phenomenon mediated by both that organization's own internal history and the available external resources (i.e., technologies). For example, computers (a technology) are resources available to the court in 1977 that were not available in 1938. The introduction of various technologies hinges upon more than availability; these introductions also depend on the receptivity of court personnel who presently control the processes of organizational activity within the bankruptcy court. Going back to the notion of contradiction, such an introduction may provide a more efficient tool for processing cases but undermine the traditional foundation of a court of law and the professional autonomy of judges. If computers are introduced it provides another example of a "more or less incomplete," not a finite, solution to ongoing organizational activity.

Thus, *organizations can be examined as formations in the process of transformation.* Organizations contain, like all historically demarcated events, contradictory solutions, "more or less incomplete" solutions, which in turn provide the dynamic forces that make them constantly changing structures. These potentially contradictory solutions may give rise to the possibility of transformation. Organizational change does not appear *de novo*; rather it must be understood as one period in the larger history of an organization.

While traditional organizational theory has consistently overlooked the distinction between processs and outcome, it nevertheless provides research strategies that may be combined in order to illuminate the relationship between the formation and the transformation of an organization.

Toward a Research Strategy for Studying the Bankruptcy Court

It is now clear that the perspectives relied upon in organizational research present a fundamental problem. Yet with clarification of this problem, by making the distinction between outcome and process, it is possible to both integrate available research strategies and carry out an analysis as a historically specific event. In moving to a concrete research situation, the concept of formation and transformation demands that we precisely specify which phases within this ongoing process are being analyzed. The delineation of the scope of the research questions demands that we be willing to reify temporarily what we have previously referred to as ongoing historical change. For without such a step the empirical examination of an organization is not possible.

We can think of organizational formation and transformation as moments within a larger history. These moments delineate parameters within which an organization must negotiate. Thus, one may examine the historical event of formation of an organization; one may examine the ongoing activities of an organization once it has been consciously created; or, one may examine the processes that give rise to the possibility of transformation. The juxtaposition of these research possibilities suggests that the empirical examination of an organization, a court for example, may give emphasis to one or another of these various phases within the larger history of that organization. In the case before us, the analysis of the bankruptcy court, emphasis is given to the empirical examination of the ongoing activity of that organization and the possibility of organizational transformation; only cursory attention is given to the specific historical process that formed the bankruptcy court.

Research into these phases of the court's history provides a means of addressing the following question: do the ongoing relationships of an organization, as specified by its history, impinge upon the possibility of transformation? In the specific case of the bankruptcy court, have the ongoing relationships of the court impinged upon the possibility of court reform? The question posed suggests the integration of two research strategies: the analysis of the bankruptcy court in its present organization, and the analysis of the process of reform of the bankruptcy court. We will describe each of these phases of research in greater detail below.

The Bankruptcy Court: 1950 to 1970

We begin with the analysis of the court as established by legislative mandate in 1938 ("Administration of the Bankruptcy Act" 1941). This mandate established formal guidelines for the organization of the bankruptcy court: (1) the jurisdiction of each court is circumscribed as the United States Federal District; (2) the private lawyers of a district will represent both the creditor and the bankrupt party, though their fees will be determined by the bankruptcy judge; (3) the tasks of the court include both consumer and corporate bankruptcy and reorganization procedures specified by the Bankruptcy Code; (4) the judges will be appointed by the respective district judges of a United States federal court; (5) the judge will be allocated one nonjudicial support person with possible additional support if granted by the Administrative Office of the United States Courts; and (6) the responsibility of this court is to determine bankruptcy cases within an equitable period of time. These guidelines provide, then, the critical issues that must be addressed in the analysis of the organizational activities of the bankruptcy court.

The jurisdiction of the bankruptcy court, as mandated in 1938, is the United States Federal District. Thus, ecological analysis, a subtheme within interorganizational research, suggests that a starting point of analysis is the aggregate characteristics of the jurisdiction relevant to the court. These aggregate characteristics include demographic and economic variables. To that end, the United States Federal District is the unit of analysis.[11] It is within the district that the 1938 Bankruptcy Act defined each court's *domain* of activities (Thompson 1967).

It is assumed that the environmental profile of a district directly affects the caseload and casemix (i.e., the task structure) as well as the development of a community of professionals who work in the bankruptcy court (i.e., the organizational matrix). Taken together, (see figure 1–2) these variables specify the *task environment* of the bankruptcy court.

The task environment is shaped by the court's environmental profile and emphasizes the openness of the boundary between the organization of the court and its larger community setting. An organization does not have a fixed or demarcated boundary such that it is possible to examine it as a circumscribed unit.

Dill speaks of the task environment of an organization as being the "stimuli to which an organization is exposed." Tasks, on the other hand, are management's "interpretation of environmental inputs" (1958, p. 43). The definitions developed in Dill's framework assume a purely behavioristic approach. Nevertheless the concept of task environment provides an anchor point for considering the gray area between purely internal and purely external dimensions of an organization under examination. That is, the task environment mediates environmental pressures and in the process interprets, categorizes, and segments the larger environment of the court into a form that the personnel of this organization are able to understand. For example, members of a stratum of the population whose work experiences make them potential consumer bankrupts become actors in a specific type of legal procedure when confronting the actual bankruptcy court; or, the lawyers of a given district become part of the "personnel" of the bankruptcy court when their livelihood revolves around such cases. Thus the purpose in delineating this level of analysis is twofold: first, to consider how the organization of the court incorporates a personnel structure that is dependent upon, but not employed by, the court itself; and second, to understand how the court organizes and translates tasks that are generated from the larger community.[12]

By contrast, size and effectiveness specify the court's *intraorganizational response* to its immediate environment, that is, its response to bankruptcy cases on the one hand and to pressures from the legal community on the other.

Size is the hub of this organization: its personnel (judicial and nonjudicial) and resources. Courts are professional, labor-intensive service organizations (Heydebrand 1977a); this means that judges (professionals) direct and carry out the service—the disposition of cases—of this court. Effectiveness is the dependent variable: when all is said and done, does the court fulfill its "goal"—the disposition and termination of bankruptcy cases? However, effectiveness is both an organizational and a political issue. The question of organizational effectiveness presents a number of problems, particularly in the case of courts where qualitative as well as quantitative indicators may be necessary to fully understand the impact of a court upon a district. Furthermore, the variable of effectiveness raises a central question: effective for whom?—the lawyers who try cases, the judges who dispose of cases, the debtors who are represented, or the administrative office of the courts that must make budget requests to Congress in order to run the court? Nevertheless, we have sought to examine the court in these terms precisely because this question must be the central issue if and when a court seeks to organizationally reform its procedures.

Each cluster of variables, then, describes various aspects of the court's formation as it is presently organized. However, each of these variables is also open to political definition, interpretation, and debate in the process of court reform. But before turning to this point, it is necessary to further consider a number of issues relevant to this phase of analysis.

While the court was mandated in 1938, examination of the organizational records suggests that the bankruptcy court in fact became a central body within the judicial branch in the post–World War II period. Moreover, the research strategy incorporates aggregate data collected by the United States Bureau of the Census; therefore, empirical analysis of the court is undertaken in 1950, in 1960, and in 1970. The 1950 period permits examination of the immediate post–World War II activities of the court; 1960 is a historical time period that permits for the examination of the court midway between the crystallization of the bankruptcy court as a significant judicial organization, 1950, and the historical time period when reform proposals emerged, 1970; finally, the 1970 time period permits for the examination of the court contemporary with the decision to investigate the present organization of the court and to determine how reform might be implemented.

Longitudinal organizational analysis presents a change dimension. However, to return to an earlier point this must be specified by historical considerations particular to the organizations under study. There are two primary ways by which the historical dimension can be specified. First, one can approach the unique event under study (e.g., a war, a revolution, a political movement, or an organization) as a single case that is to be studied through time but in isolation from other like events.[13] Second, one can approach the event as a specimen of a larger historical type (Kolko 1967; Moore 1966). In this case, comparisons are made at points in time and reliance is placed upon the comparison of specimens to yield generalizable statements—about either revolutions, wars, political movements, or organizations. (See Kennedy and Seron 1975.)

Stinchcombe (1965) suggests that the age of an organization may explain, in part, its organizational solutions. For example, older organizations may come to rely upon certain organizational technologies that were available or popular at the time of the organization's establishment. Although it may not be possible to begin longitudinal analysis at the time of formation of an organization (i.e., its establishment), particularly in the case of older types of organizations such as courts or schools, it is possible to begin analysis at a critical time of sudden growth, expansion, technological innovation, or significantly increased demand. In other words, the age of an organizational problem can be used as a guide in selecting time points of comparability. For example, in the analysis of the bankruptcy court, 1950, the post–World War II period, is the first point of analysis of the court. It is in this period that the demands of the court began to increase significantly (see chapter 3). While the court is in fact older, the earlier period is not of direct relevance to the particular problems under investigation.

However, economic, social, and demographic processes may change over time and affect the ways in which an organization functions. And, as the social structure surrounding an organization changes, so, too, do the strategies found in organizations. However, these strategies can change only to the extent permitted by the court's formation; thus, as in the case of this court it may be forced fundamentally to alter its structure: the ongoing organizational demands on the court may come into conflict with its present formation. But this process of change is complicated by the very practical fact that this present organization has supported the development of an entrenched, though traditional, elite, an elite whose interests are not served, necessarily, by organizational changes and innovations. Hence, "it is the resistance of established social relations to adaptation to the everchanging forces of production which creates the dynamic of social and organizational contradictions" (Heydebrand 1977a, p. 87). It is the task of this research to examine if this is in fact the case in the reform of the bankruptcy court.

Reform of the Bankruptcy Court

Each cluster of variables that describes the court's present organization is open for political debate in the process of reform. Thus, for example the organizational matrix—the presence and necessity of lawyers and trustees—becomes a debatable and political point; so, too, with the issue of task demands, judicial personnel and resources, and effectiveness. The reform debate of the court is not merely a discussion of the day-to-day addition of tasks, personnel, or machines, but rather it is the consideration and examination of the ways in which the nexuses of these tasks, persons, and machines might be fundamentally relinked, reapportioned, and reallocated. That is, the analysis of court reform is the analysis of organizational transformation: reform of the bankruptcy court poses, then, the political possibility of change in the court's organizational structure.

The question then arises: who debates these issues of court reform? As Weber suggests, organizational change is a struggle for power between strata that have in the past, or seek in the future, to control organizations through the "apex" of bureaucratic formations. Relating this struggle over change to a court setting, Bendix suggests that "the legal order possesses a 'specialized personnel' for the implementation of coercive power (enforcement machines: priests, judges, police, the military, etc.) and the conventional order does not" (1962, p. 390). That is, the history of a court defines a demarcated group whose responsibility it is to "enforce" the "rules"or laws of that society. For example, in the context of bankruptcy, this group has historically included judges, lawyers, trustees, and court administrators. So those who participate in this reform debate represent various groups within the legal order.

But a second question also arises: do these groups within the legal order have equal political power to influence the process of reform? Is reform of a court debated by groups who form a "community of equals?" This question opens a Pandora's box concerning the definition of interest group in a democratic society. Fortunately, this debate has been adequately summarized by others (Alford 1975; Balbus 1971, 1972; Bachrach and Baratz 1962; Connolly 1972; Giddens 1973; Lowi 1969; O'Connor 1975; Offe 1972a; Rogin 1970; Wolfe 1973; Wolff 1968; Wolin 1960). (But also see Bentley 1908; Flathman 1966; Schubert 1960; Truman 1951.) However, it is necessary to address the above question for the purposes of this study. In a word, the debate concerning reform of this court, like the debate of all political issues in American society, is *not* carried out by groups who form a "community of equals."

While there are those who suggest that there is no connection between economic position and political influence, the "opportunity [to influence policy] is limited by the group's structural position within the stratification of society" (Mills 1963, p. 316). Insofar as the United States is a class-based society, so its political debates are also class based (Balbus 1971; Offe 1972a, 1972b; Wolff 1968).

This is not to suggest, however, that a pluralist ideology of equals is an unimportant force in American political life. In fact, its power is remarkable, as it affects both the "theory" of how American society "works" (Hurst 1950), as well as the "practice" of how social science has "studied" that society (Gouldner 1970; Lowi 1969). And in the chapters that follow, the resilience of a class-based ideology of democratic pluralism is repeatedly revealed.

Given the force of this ideology, how is it possible to understand the subtleties and innuendos of political debate? Wolff (1968) suggests that the study of political power is two-pronged: is the issue under debate an object of anyone's decision and who decides it? In other words, political issues themselves describe the priorities of a society. The description and issues of political debate cannot be separated from those groups who seek to affect the outcome of reform. "Interest groups" become active around issues; but not all interest groups have equal input into this outcome. "*Political* power, then, can best be understood as the power to make and enforce decisions with regard to matters of major social importance" (Wolff 1968, p. 93).

Hence, it is necessary to consider both a group's position vis-à-vis the issue under debate, that is, their "objective" position as well as what and how they contribute to that debate, that is, their "subjective" position (Balbus 1971, 1972). However, both objective and subjective interests are historically specific questions for analysis. Therefore, a group's "objective" interest is not weak or powerful, as the case may be, out of time and place, but rather, weak or powerful precisely because that group (e.g., judges, lawyers, creditors, etc.) is part of a social and historical period. Understood in this context, it becomes apparent that the organizational analysis of the bankruptcy court in 1950, 1960, and 1970 provides a relatively objective and historically specific backdrop for the political debates of court reform; it provides a point of departure for clarifying the relationship between a particular interest group's stated (i.e., subjective) position and its historical function vis-à-vis the development and structure of this organization. Since "taking attitudes as the starting point precludes any systematic specification of the determinants of attitudes" (Balbus 1971, p. 160), the "determinants of attitudes" must always be examined in a historical context (Balbus 1972). Returning to an earlier point, an organization is the historical outcome of "conscious, practical activity." And the conscious, practical dimension of that activity becomes clear only if the political, social, and economic determinants of an interest group's attitudes are also considered.

The possibility of change, then, is both an outgrowth of an organization's history and a political challenge to that formation since some interest groups may consciously demand more radical alternatives. After all, "language is also one of the most creative, innovative, demystifying and liberative aspects of human practical activity" (Heydebrand 1977a, p. 85). That is, the forces of change surface when some groups demand greater control or reform within the organization's milieu. However, the political power to effect the desired outcome remains a historical possibility mediated by the complexities of the organization's present social relations.

As court reform is a political debate, so it may actually become many debates. That is, many organizational "solutions" may be posed as alternative strategies by various interest groups. Moreover, once solutions, i.e., policies, are posed, "the age of social innocence is lost, and from that moment any decision, *including the decision to do nothing,* is a deliberate policy for which the authors of the decision can be held responsible" (Wolff 1968, p. 92; emphasis added). We must begin with an understanding of which groups pose a solution, a policy, and of each group's position in the overall structure and history of the court.

Taken together, the analysis of the development and the reform of an organization is the analysis of a specific moment in that organization's history. A stratum, a fraction of a class, or an interest group, can use an organization to gain further control over a limited resource. At the moment of transformation, the structure of relations among strata comes to the fore in the question: how do various interest groups (strata) seek to control, for their own ends, the organization under consideration? It is in the process of reform, an "atypical" moment in an organization's history, that the "typical" or given class relations of that organization may be elucidated. Insofar as an organization, and particularly a court, provides a setting for the meeting of various strata, it is possible to examine who the organization serves by empirically examining political dialogue at the point of the atypical, or at the moment when the organization seeks to transform its structure. However, transformation is not an isolated moment; rather, reform must be examined in the historical context and in light of the forces that pushed specific groups to demand or resist change. Thus, the analysis of this atypical moment must be couched in a diachronic perspective—ongoing organizational activity.

Let us turn then to the various proposals and interest groups of court reform.

The Proposed Reforms

In part, the post–Civil War period has been characterized by a movement toward bureaucratization but in the name of administrative reform (see Bendix and Roth 1971; Kolko 1963, 1976; McConnell 1966; Weinstein 1968). The historical emergence of this change in bureaucratic structures assumes that "public officials" must be administrators for a national citizenry—or the total polity (Weber 1946a). This study provides, then, a case study of a larger theme in American history: the possibility of legal rational bureaucratization in the name of social reform.

The introduction asserted that the reform of this court revolves around two antithetical solutions. The impetus of each proposal itself underscores the point made earlier, that bureaucratization is neither inevitable nor irreversible. For purposes of discussion, these proposals will be referred to as the *Commission's Bill* and the *Judges' Bill.*

The Commission's Bill: Discussions of reform of the bankruptcy court were initiated in 1970 with a congressional resolution that established a commission of experts to investigate the court (S.J. Res. 88). In this early stage in the reform process a crucial political issue was brought forward: judges in bankruptcy court were eliminated from the commission. The Judges' Bill is a response to this early decision by the Congress. The chapters that follow reveal that the judges consistently argued that the Commission's Bill overlooked important issues that the Judges' Bill addressed.

The major suggestions of this commission resulted in a bill that is now being debated (see *Report of the Commission on Bankruptcy Laws,* 1973). The suggestions are the following:

1. The establishment of an administrative agency, housed in the Executive, to process bankruptcy cases. This agency would operate through local and regional offices. The employees of these agencies would become a part of the civil service. The administration would handle all services presently performed by the judge in bankruptcy and trustees in the liquidation of cases. In addition to these services, this agency would provide counselling to debtors to avoid future bankruptcy.

2. The establishment of a bankruptcy court that would hear those controversies not settled by the administrative agency. The jurisdiction of these courts would not necessarily coincide with that of the federal district courts. These courts would have the right to use juries if and when necessary. Appeals from the court would proceed to the U.S. District Court.

3. All bankruptcy proceedings would be the responsibility of this agency and court, with the exception of railroad reorganization cases, which would remain under the auspices of the United States District Court.

4. All bankruptcy cases (consumer and business) would be filed with the administrative agency and proceed to the bankruptcy court only if a controversy arises.

In broad outline, the Commission's Bill seeks to streamline bankruptcy procedure by eliminating a courthouse hearing when it is unnecessary. Though trustees and lawyers would be available, they would be used only when absolutely necessary. However, the legal options of "straight" bankruptcy and plans of reorganization for both business and consumer debtors would still be available.

The Judges' Bill: The Judges' Bill is, of course, the direct response to the Commission's Bill. Its rationale rests upon the fact that judges in bankruptcy were excluded from the investigations and proposals of the commission. Nevertheless, the political aspect of this counter-bill cannot be overlooked. The major suggestions of this bill are the following:

1. The establishment of a bankruptcy court, separate and distinct from the United States District Court, to hear all cases in bankruptcy. That is, the proposed court would have jurisdiction over railroad reorganization cases as well as all other bankruptcy cases. "Only in the Judges' Bill is the goal a one-stop, full-service bankruptcy court" (Lee 1975, p. 6) for all types of bankruptcy cases. That is, both consumer and business cases would commence in this new court. Appeals from the court would proceed to the U.S. Circuit Court of Appeals.

2. The Branch of Bankruptcy, a part of the Judiciary, would be supported by appropriated funds. The director of this new branch within the judiciary would be responsible for adopting rules and regulations; appointing trustees, lawyers, creditors, and auctioneers; acting as the disbursing agent for funds of

bankrupt estates; assisting individuals with the filing of bankruptcy petitions; and introducing data processing techniques where feasible.

3. The role of trustees, lawyers, and creditors in the bankruptcy process would be maintained and formalized through the Branch of Bankruptcy. Fees for such services, particularly legal services, would be set by the director in consultation with the local bar. The first meeting of creditors would remain a feature of all bankruptcy proceedings with the option of electing a trustee at the close of this meeting.

Thus, the Judges' Bill seeks to "professionalize" the bankruptcy court. The thrust of this bill seeks to legitimate the elements that have shaped the organization of the court.

While there are points of agreement in the two bills the points of difference are dramatic and suggest antithetical solutions to the present problems of the court. However, the rationale for supporting one or another of these reforms rests with an interest group's position in the present court, and the gains or losses to be made through supporting one or another of these proposals.

The scope of the respective proposals demands that we reconsider the political implications of the variables that have circumscribed the court's history and development. Reconsideration of the *task structure* of the court addresses the type of laws or rules that will guide the interpretation of bankruptcy procedure: should the law remain substantive, based upon individual case interpretation, or should the law be made formal, based upon more rational and specific rules? That is, should the structure of tasks of the present court become rules to complement a bureaucratic agency or should they remain laws that must be individually interpreted by a judge with formal training?

Reconsideration of the *organizational matrix* addresses the relationship of lawyers and trustees with the bankruptcy court: should the members of the organizational matrix—the legal community of the bankruptcy court—be eliminated, where possible, from bankruptcy procedure to complement a bureaucratic agency, or should they be maintained, in all cases, to complement a fully autonomous bankruptcy court?

Reconsideration of the *size and resources* of the bankruptcy court addresses the debate over a professional or a bureaucratic alternative in the process of reform. Should the court become a bureaucratic agency housed in the executive branch of government, or a fully autonomous collegial organization of the judicial branch of government?

Finally, reconsideration of *effectiveness* of the court raises two questions in the process of reform: what social, political, and economic factors have caused the court to become ineffective? And, what specific services (for example, new laws, educational services, computers, etc.) might be introduced to make the court effective in the future?

There are two formal proposals to reform the court. However, there is a third possibility—that the court will remain as it is presently organized. Each issue of court reform contains this possibility. The focus of this study is on the

Commission's Bill and the Judges' Bill; however, consideration will also be given to this third possibility—one that Wolff suggests cannot be overlooked.

The Interest Groups of Reform

The final decision on reform will be made by the Congress and signed by the president. Therefore this analysis examines a judicial organization—the court—confronting a political legislative organization—the Congress—over the issue of court reform.

In the case of the bankruptcy court, interest groups have been both "insiders" and "outsiders" (Merton 1966) to the court's development. Insiders fall into four groups: judges, practicing attorneys, creditors and bankers, and the representative of the Bankruptcy Division of the Administrative Office of the United States Courts—those who have been part of the court's day-to-day history and development. Outsiders are made up of representatives of organized labor, legal scholars, public-interest law groups, and representatives of the United States Attorney's Office—those who have not been part of the court's day-to-day activities. Debates over court reform highlight the relationship between various groups' positions in the development of the court and their attitude towards the issues of court reform: which proposal do they support and what are the implications of that position?[14]

Not all groups are interested in all aspects of reform. While some are concerned with the question of the redefinition of laws, others address the question of the professional or bureaucratic reform alternative. Which issues these groups address is as important as what they say about the issues themselves. That is, the scope of a group's orientation toward reform itself clarifies why and for whom such processes of change may be implemented.

Conclusion

The task of this chapter has been to present a perspective for the organizational analysis of the bankruptcy court. We examined both relevant classical and contemporary questions within organizational theory. More specifically, as the classical basis of organizational research, Weber's questions demand consideration of issues often ignored in both longitudinal and interorganizational research. Whereas interorganizational analysis is, by definition, a political question, the empirical research conducted in this area has consistently skirted the issue. Longitudinal analysis has also ignored political issues insofar as the empirical research has examined trends within organizations without reference to the impetus for or initiation of change.

The analysis that follows seeks to integrate these above perspectives. In so doing, we hope to move the area of organizational research in a direction that more closely complements its classical origins by paying particular attention to the *political implications of the development of the court* as well as to the factors that push toward reform within that court. Hence, a central issue in the analysis of organizations must be the role of rationalization, although this is not to assume that this process is inevitable or absolute. Rather, the direction of change within an organization is a subject that must be investigated through reliance upon empirical data and through the investigation of historical factors that shape the particular organization. Let us turn then to Chapter 3 and an examination of the organizational and political dimension of this court's caseload and casemix.

Notes

1. Derived from the concept of power that involves imposition of will, domination is defined as the "manifested will (*command*) of the *ruler* or *rulers* . . . meant to influence the conduct of one or more others (the *ruled*) and actually does influence it in such a way that their conduct to a socially relevant degree occurs as if the ruled had made the content of the command the maxim of their conduct for its very own sake" (Weber 1954, p. 328).

2. Weber's earliest research on the Protestant Ethic lays the foundation for the argument that permeates all of his work, that is, that the transition from the Calvinist ethic of work to the capitalist ethic of rational work rests upon the social translation of the calling; discipline; formal obligation to work; a distrust of emotions; and a commitment to God's plan. This results in a secular, methodical responsibility to a higher order, the bureaucratic apparatus.

3. Collegiality involves one type of rational authority. However, its structure of reporting to a hierarchy is based upon control by a "ruler" rather than by a bureaucratic official; in this sense, collegial organization is, relative to monocratic bureaucracy, not as rational (see Weber 1946a).

4. Insofar as rational bureaucracy is an ideal-type construct, organizations, in their day-to-day relations, can and often do manifest traditional and charismatic dimensions. Rational bureaucratic control, therefore, refers to only one aspect of organizational coordination (Heydebrand 1973a, pp. 81-82).

5. The historical development of the official within the organization coincides with and defines a specific type of worker relationship. While Marx's first concern is with understanding how the worker is attached to his work place, Weber is primarily concerned with understanding what characterizes the modern work situation. According to Weber, official appointments through examination or through formal procedural rules define the criteria for selection to specific office. This very particular definition of course mirrors both the German and American civil service where jobs are allotted on the basis of examination. Within each grade a demarcated number of steps specifies the possi-

ble degree of upward mobility. In other words, mobility becomes a given aspect of the contemporary work experience, but is limited to steps within a grade. Thus an official who is selected on the basis of personal or collegial criteria falls outside the bureaucratic model. For example, judges in a court, be they elected to office or appointed by an elected official, are not bureaucratic officials despite the fact that they must have expert (i.e., legal) training in order to be considered for appointment.

6. We are left, however, with a complicated contradiction in Weber's work. On the one hand, Weber assumes that there will be protest from the old guard in the process of transition. On the other hand, Weber's writings reflect a profound pessimism which assumes that ever-increasing rationalization (i.e., calculation, planning, formal authority, and rules) will, by definition, come to characterize the western world. There is therefore, an assumption of struggle, but, simultaneously, and perhaps more importantly, an assumption that the struggle will terminate in favor of the rationalizing alternative.

As Bendix points out, "types" of domination are not, in fact, present in society in their pure, or ideal-typical, form; therefore, inquiry must be simultaneously guided by "the recurrent issues that characterize the struggle for power;" that is, the analysis of struggle for power must be a historically informed research, a research resting upon the concrete issues and dynamics of a particular problem (Bendix 1962, p. 329).

7. Thompson's (1967) work opened up an avenue of theoretical concern for interorganizational research. The concept of *domain of an organization*, elucidated by Thompson, specifies the points at which an organization is dependent upon, and therefore must negotiate with, its larger environment. *Domain consensus* is a dialogue between an organization and its environment that results in establishment of control over technologies and resources that are not intraorganizationally controlled. Thompson presents a typology of dependence upon the domain of an organization that moves from coopting (see Selznick 1966) to contracting to coalescing. The analysis of domain consensus revolves around *political questions*, meaning that the direction an organization takes, as a social actor, in controlling aspects of its domain entails a "struggle for power" (to use Weber's term). As the work has moved forward empirically it has relied upon the concept of "organizational linkages." Through this concept, attention is focused on the degree to which an organization is coopting, contracting, or coalescing. For example Pfeffer (1972) focuses on the concept of cooptation in his study of hospital boards of directors and indicates that this is one way of gaining control over the hospital's environment. Pfeffer is concerned to show that "coopting" the board of directors is one alternative the hospital can use for handling its organizational tasks. Zald (1969) has posited a number of very interesting questions concerning the role of boards of directors in various types of organizations and suggests an interesting direction for examining interorganizational relations. Board power may be specified by a number of variables:

knowledge, resources, status, and sex. Given these various sources of board power, he asks what types of organizations demand boards that are active in the internal operations of an organization as opposed to the external relations of an organization. At what points in the "life-cycle" of an organization do boards take a more active role? Pfeffer's analysis of hospitals is an empirical study using a number of Zald's suggestions.

This introduces an important question not commonly considered in other organizational analyses. By extending the focus on analysis beyond the boundaries of the organization, the question of political struggle immediately arises as an issue of concern. Unfortunately, despite its obvious relevance, few studies have, in fact, taken up this question of political struggle.

8. Another avenue of theoretical concern for interorganizational analysis has been the relationship between ecological factors and organizational relations. The ecologists argue that aggregate characteristics of a region provide a frame of reference for organizations and that this framework sets limits on the forms that social organization may assume (Duncan and Schnore 1959). Taken one step further, the demography of a region relevant to an organization itself becomes a part of that organization's structure. The introduction of demographic, ecological, and economic characteristics relevant to an organization breaks the boundaries between that organization and its larger environment. Noell (1974), for example, uses the American states as his unit of analysis and draws upon demographic indicators as the predictive variable in the analysis of the size and complexity of government bureaucracies. The extension of this analysis demands consideration of such questions as whether the numbers and types of firms in an area are as much a "part" of an organization as the actual tasks the organization processes. Heydebrand (1973a) points out that the "structural differentiation" of an area and the "task structure" of an organization should not be seen as distinguishing a fixed and absolute boundary; rather, taken together, they should be considered as "dialelectically related points of reference."

9. The dimensions of the social structure external to an organization should be considered broadly. As Stinchcombe (1965) points out, external considerations should include groups, institutions, laws, population characteristics, and sets of social relations. Given this broader conceptual framework, Stinchcombe also argues that organizations are one of the few locales where varying social classes meet, and that therefore an organization can be a major determinant of class relations. This observation reflects the Weberian (1946b) position that social strata are organized around *various* activities. However, social classes can also *use* organizations as a tool to gain further control over limited resources. In other words, interorganizational relations must address the complex problem of class relations as they are played out in the formation of an organization. We must remain sensitive to the question: for whom is the organization an effective structure?

10. The work of Hannan and Freeman (1975) on school districts presents

a complex picture. Their findings support the claim that administrative-personnel ratios are comprised of complex aggregates of data that cross-sectional data alone may not unearth. Emphasis upon the examination of administrative-personnel ratios is itself an outgrowth of Weberian considerations. Originally developed by Bendix (1963) to specify the narrow concept of bureaucratization, the term was operationalized as the proportion of salaried administrative personnel only. On a more general level, Hannan and Freeman suggest that "when demand is increasing, the size of the direct component [contact with students] increases as does the supportive component [no contact with students]. But when demand declines, the loss in direct component is not matched by loss in the supportive component. That is, the supportive component tends to increase on the upswings but decreases less on the downswings" (p. 227).

The concept of upswings and downswings raises an interesting problem not directly considered in their analysis: what gives rise to upswings and downswings in terms of enrollments, teachers, support staff, and so on? Are there political, ecological, or demographic factors that help to explain the patterns of these changes? The relatively recent and limited developments of longitudinal analysis have not addressed this important consideration. While Hannan and Freeman's work may reflect a significant advance over earlier work, it still does not explain the origins of upswings and downswings.

11. See Appendix A for a further discussion of the steps involved in this procedure.

12. It should be pointed out that there have been numerous tactics taken in organizational research in an attempt to specify the concept of environment of an organization. Kriesberg's (1968) work on international peace nongovernmental associations assumes that the role of these types of organizations is in part shaped by the national differences in the member states, in this case the U.S. and the U.S.S.R. As a general hypothesis, Kriesberg argues that the basic conflict in national outlook of the U.S. and the U.S.S.R. will tend to favor a situation in which the U.S. and the U.S.S.R. will not participate in the same organizations involved with peace keeping. It can be seen in this study that environment refers to the governmental structure of a society that determines the type of international voluntary associations available. Lieberson and Allen (1963) in their study of the location of voluntary associations hypothesize that locating the headquarters of an organization is influenced by ecological considerations of an area. They use purely demographic characteristics to operationalize the unit to be examined. In addition, to the extent that they are concerned with the influences that determine the location of headquarters, they work with a more inductive model of inference. Pugh, Hickson, et al. (1969) have developed the concept of "contextual variables" to take account of environmental considerations. Here they argue that "it is not a model of organization in an environment, but a separation of variables of structure and of organizational performance from other variables commonly hypothesized to be related

to them, which we called 'contextual' in the sense that they can be regarded as settings within which structure is developed" (p. 92). Thus, contextual variables include origin and history, ownership and control, size, charter, technology, and so on. It can be seen from this brief review of a number of studies that a growing theme in organizational research has been a concern with including data that circumscribe and articulate the milieu within which an organization must perform.

13. The early case studies by Gouldner (1955) and Selznick (1966) are explorations of the history and development of one particular organization examined in isolation from other organizations that may have exhibited similar patterns. These analyses can be viewed as community studies insofar as the boundaries between the organization and larger community are not treated as rigid. Many aspects of these early studies rely upon community factors to explain specific organizational developments and strategies.

14. See Appendix B for a further discussion of how these data were analyzed.

3

Increasing Demand, Backlog, and the Need for Change

The bankruptcy court has the authority to decide legal disputes. The demands and complexities of these bankruptcy disputes may pose an organizational strain for the personnel of the court; new organizational processes may be advocated to "correct" this strain. Thus in the process of reform the definition of the demands and complexities of bankruptcy disputes becomes an issue open for debate. This chapter will examine the relationship between the organizational and political dimensions of the caseload and casemix of this court.

The bankruptcy court is a professional organization, that is, it is a special type of work organization in which there is a specification of tasks and a developed knowledge base, and where the employed professionals have control over resources (Freidson 1972; Heydebrand and Noell 1973). There are problems in this last matter in that professionals in courts (i.e., judges), do not directly control their own resources.[1] Judges do, however, specify the task structure of the organization, and direct and carry out their work on the basis of prior training. Therefore, the adjudication of cases, or the administration of legal questions, is done by judges trained to implement (adjudicate and administer) the law.[2]

The law is translated into the task structure of the court and defines several features of court activity; for example, it answers the questions: What is a legal dispute? What type of legal dispute is involved? What court should hear the dispute? And what are the guidelines for acting upon the legal dispute? However, the specialization within law, and in particular bankruptcy law, circumscribes several of these task considerations (Parness 1973; Schubert 1960). That is, bankruptcy law delineates the nature of a bankruptcy dispute, describes the court that hears such cases, and determines guidelines for resolving cases.

From the perspective of organizational analysis, the task structure defines what the organization does. To the extent that legal cases, the task structure of the organization, can be routinized, the law itself can be formalized and rationalized—a position advocated by some reformers.

The Caseload and Casemix of the Bankruptcy Court: 1930 to 1970

Organizationally, the task structure includes the caseload, or demand, and the casemix, or complexity of tasks of the court. The first factor in the calculus of reform is the composition of demands on the court. How have these demands changed? What accounts for these developments? And, how are these "quantitative" factors translated into political debate by various interest groups in the process of reform?

Table 3-1a
The Demands of the Bankruptcy Court

	Total Demand	
1930	124,000	
1940	107,000	
1950	64,000	
1960	192,300	
1970	373,100	

	Filings	% of Total
1930	62,800	51
1940	52,000	49
1950	33,400	52
1960	110,000	57
1970	194,400	52

	Pending	% of Total
1930	61,400	49
1940	55,000	51
1950	30,600	48
1960	82,300	43
1970	178,700	48

Demand is a relatively straightforward aspect of the task structure. In the case of the bankruptcy court, it refers to the total demand on the court in any given year. Since a case can come before the court at any point during the course of a year, the demand includes all commenced and pending cases. Table 3-1a shows the total demand, filings, and pending cases before the bankruptcy court from 1930 to 1970. It is clear that all three measures have increased markedly. But the most significant factor is the growing backlog—or pending cases—in the court. That is, the growth in the absolute share of pending cases suggests one reason why the personnel of the court may be increasingly unable to keep pace with the demand for court services.

Since the bankruptcy court is a specialized organization, it handles only those cases that involve bankruptcy issues. Specialization, by definition, circumscribes the variety of tasks within this court. However, a basic dimension of the variability of cases is generated by the distinction made between consumer and corporate cases. That is, the variety of tasks that come before the bankruptcy court can be reduced to two basic categories.

Table 3-1b
The Complexity of Bankruptcy Cases

	Asset Cases	%
1950	3,800	11
1960	10,500	10
1970	22,400	12

	Business Cases (Chapters X and XI)	%
1950	700	2
1960	700	6
1970	900	5

	Consumer Cases (Chapter XIII)	%
1950	6,000	18
1960	13,600	12
1970	28,900	15

The complexity of the task structure refers to such questions as which of the cases that come before the court are nonroutinized work processes and, as a result, tend to demand a greater length of time in court, require greater resources of the court, and involve possible conflicts over the decisions made? In this research the variety of tasks have been divided into two basic categories, consumer and corporate cases. Within each of these categories, particular types of cases generate more or less complex demands. In the case of consumer bankruptcies, Chapter XIII proceedings of the Bankruptcy Code refer to a reorganization or plan of payment for the consumer bankrupt. If individuals use this legal procedure, they turn over their earnings to a trustee hired by the court and this trustee supervises, for a designated period of time, the payment of debt. With this procedure, the consumer, rather than liquidating all those debts that are dischargeable under a given state's statutes, makes an arrangement within the court that assures payment to creditors. The decision to use this legal procedure rather than straight bankruptcy means that the case will tend to remain within the jurisdiction of the court for a longer period of time, and will therefore require a greater proportion of the judge's time as well as the time of clerks in the processing of legal papers. Table 3-1b shows the number of Chapter XIII—consumer reorganization—cases filed in the bankruptcy court from 1950 to 1970. It is clear that such cases are increasing through time and hence may be posing more demands for the court's services.

Corporate bankruptcies tend to be more complex procedures. A primary distinction between consumer and corporate bankruptcies is seen in the fact that corporate bankruptcy cases are more likely to involve assets or monies either in liquid form or tied up in the bankrupt business. Therefore, corporate cases commonly involve the distribution of assets to creditors and the conflicts that may arise between various parties. Table 3-1b reveals that the absolute number of asset cases clearly increased over the decades since 1950; however, the relative number (percent) of such cases stayed basically the same.

Chapter X and XI cases of corporate bankruptcy allow for the rearrangement of a business enterprise in an attempt to keep the business afloat. That is, the bankruptcy court does not handle only cases where bankruptcy and the resulting distribution of money to creditors generated by the sale of a business is the alternative. An important "goal" of this court is to provide a "fresh start" to both consumer and corporate bankrupts. The goal of a fresh start is built into the legal doctrine in that a business may come before the court, declare its financial situation as precarious, and use the auspices of the court to liquidate debts, establish a plan of payment of debts, and hopefully reestablish a firm foundation so as to continue as a viable business.[3]

The size of the business, the nature of its operations, the seriousness of its financial state, the the viability of regaining solvency all enter into the complexity of a particular case before the court. Nevertheless, the decision to attempt a Chapter X or XI proceeding means, by definition, a more complex legal procedure than a straight corporate bankruptcy that involves the sale of property and the distribution of realized monies to creditors. In comparison to the absolute number of asset and consumer cases, business reorganization procedures have remained a miniscule share of the court's workload. Paradoxically, however, they are perhaps the most important bankruptcy procedure insofar as they may affect the economy of a region. Thus, it will be important to determine which, if any, factors explain business bankruptcy cases.

For all three types of cases—asset, business, and consumer—the relative share of such work has remained rather stable; thus, most cases that come before this court have been "straight," no-asset bankruptcies (Shuchman 1971). If the relative share of "complex" cases has not changed then it follows that the court's problem may be rather straightforward—simply too much work. But is it in fact this simple? Do business interests, for example, exert a disproportionate influence on the formation and transformation of the bankruptcy court? In sum, there are two dimensions to the tasks of the bankruptcy court: first, the demand or the caseload (that is, pending, filing, demand) of the court; and second, the complexity of tasks or the distinction between consumer (that is, Chapter XIII) cases, asset cases, and business cases (that is, Chapter X and XI).

The Environment of the Bankruptcy Court

Clearly, the number and complexity of bankruptcy cases has increased at a rather marked pace. Why is this so? The structural dimensions that lead to these cases of economic failure are the result of dynamic changes in the political economy and must in part be seen as the result of a competitive network that defines a capitalist enterprise. It is beyond the scope of this study to analyze the causes of bankruptcy.[4] However, it is within the domain of this study to clarify what trends might cause an increase in the number of bankruptcy cases, since this increase is pointed to by some interest groups as proof of the need for reform. According to O'Connor, "The relationship between monopoly capital and organized labor is the dominant production relation or social relation of production in United States society" (1973, pp. 64–65).[5] The monopoly sector directs economic development through large-scale production and through an organized labor force that receives relatively high wages. The marriage of organized labor and monopoly capital is based upon their mutual need for an increasingly central role of the state and for the introduction of labor-saving technologies.

The dominance of the monopoly sector is embedded in its relation to the state sector (Heilbroner 1965; Kolko 1976; Williams 1961; Weinstein 1968). Moreover, today the state produces its own goods and services and contracts with the private monopoly sector. To use O'Connor's term, the ongoing negotiation between the state and monopoly sectors is moving in the direction of a "social-industrial complex." "The . . . only practical long-run option available to the state is to encourage productivity in the monopoly sector (to restrain costs and prices and increase production and profits) and in the state sector (to ameliorate the fiscal crisis)" (O'Connor 1973, p. 51).

By contrast, the competitive sector is composed of small-scale production units for local markets. Whereas the monopoly sector rests upon high ratio of capital to labor with high productivity, the reverse is true of the competitive sector: it is described by the small businesses, restaurants, and stores that dot the continent:

Capitalism is in part the history of peasants and farmers, home owners, petty craftsmen and tradesmen, and others forced into poverty by the advance of capitalist agriculture, factory production, mass retailing, and so on; in part the history of industries and entire regions becoming economically impoverished as a result of changes in technology and market forces; in part the history of poverty generated by recession and depressions and by particular industrial and occupational structures that confine some people to low-income, unstable employment. (O'Connor 1973, p. 158)

Unlike monopoly industries, competitives businesses remain subject to the inflationary cycles of capitalist development that limit wages and productivity (Leontief 1968).

Merger is a common tool of the monopoly sector but having effects also upon the competitive sector. Depending upon circumstances, the merger can be used as a tax write-off, as a way to gain access to government contracts, as a way to gain access to technical know-how; as a way to integrate production and distribution facilities horizontally and vertically, as a way to diversify with fewer risks, and as a way to keep up corporate growth rates (O'Connor 1974). But the effect of such buying and selling among the giants does not stop with this sector: "The extensive (as contrasted with intensive) character of monopoly capital growth not only generates more unemployment in competitive industries (surplus labor) but also liquidates large numbers of small businesses (surplus capitalists)" (O'Connor 1973, p. 29; also see Pfeffer 1972; Gort 1962). The firm itself, the locus of economic activity, becomes a commodity in the monopoly-dominated phase of capitalist development.

The competitive sector of the economy is subservient to the emerging "social-industrial complex." However, the competitive sector employs approximately one-third of the labor force, composed of unskilled, unorganized minority employees.[6] The employers within the competitive sector are perhaps most directly, over the long haul, subject to corporate bankruptcy. Unlike those in the monopoly sector, competitive-sector industries tend to have less direct access to the executive branch and thus less control over economic planning and development (Auerbach 1976; Horwitz 1977; Unger 1976). However, to the extent that competitive sector firms are more likely to go bankrupt, the court in part "legitimates" and maintains this sector of the economy. After all, the stated goal of a bankruptcy procedure is to allow the debtor a fresh start.

Thus, the caseload and casemix of this court are in part shaped by *industrial fluctuations of the competitive sector and the merger activity of the monopoly sector.* Tables 3–2 and 3–3 show zero-order (r) correlations between selected measures of the monopoly and competitive sectors with each aspect of the court's caseload and casemix in 1950, 1960, and 1970. These findings clearly reveal that these sectors of the economy are associated with the court's demand in the post–World War II period. Moreover, the strength of these associations varies with the different measures of the caseload of the court.

Thus, the number of mergers reveals a particularly strong association with business reorganization cases in both 1960 (r = .81) and 1970 (r = .85). (Note that data for 1950 are not available.) The monopolization of industrial spheres has the inevitable effect of forcing some businesses into corporate reorganization, and possible bankruptcy.

The competitive sector is measured by manufacturing, mining, and agriculture.[7] Manufacturing closely represents a traditionally competitive sphere whereas both mining and agriculture have increasingly become monopoly-controlled and hence subject to government regulation and "protection" (Offe 1972a). For example in agriculture, between 1950 and 1965 output expanded by 45 percent whereas employment (unskilled) dropped by 45 percent. So competitive sector agriculture is today composed of few, labor-intensive, low-production farms. Not surprisingly then, agricultural measures exhibit a stronger association with filings and demand in 1950 than in 1970; it seems that agribusiness need no longer rely upon the auspices of this court for protection.

Table 3-2
Zero-Order Correlations (Pearson's r) between Size of Task and Bankruptcy Court Environment in 1950, 1960, and 1970

	Pending			Filings			Demand		
	'50	'60	'70	'50	'60	'70	'50	'60	'70
Monopoly sector									
Mergers (#)	—	.40	.36	—	.49	.41	—	.47	.39
Assets ($)	—	—	−.04	—	.02	−.02	—	.01	−.03
Competitive sector									
Manufacturing	.09	.41	.39	.41	.44	.44	.42	.45	.43
Mining	—	.06	.28	—	.10	.30	—	.08	.30
Agriculture	−.08	—	.23	.40	—	.25	.39	—	.24
White collar									
# White collar	—	.21	.25	—	.23	.28	—	.23	.27
# Govt. employees	—	.43	.66	—	.43	.65	—	.45	.67
Median education	−.05	.13	.16	−.28	.19	.22	−.15	.17	.19
Median income	—	−.05	.20	−.15	.02	.26	−.28	−.01	.23
Savings capital	—	.24	.71	—	.28	.80	—	.28	.77
Demographic patterns									
Population size	.07	.15	.64	.52	.16	.64	.52	.16	.65
Population density	.13	.16	.20	.11	.16	.19	.13	.16	.20
Net migration	—	.26	.57	—	.38	.57	—	.34	.58

Table 3-3
Zero-Order Correlations (Pearson's r) between Task Complexity and Bankruptcy Court Environment in 1950, 1960, and 1970

	Asset cases			Business cases			Consumer cases		
	'50	'60	'70	'50	'60	'70	'50	'60	'70
Monopoly sector									
Mergers (#)	—	.46	.35	—	.81	.85	—	−.05	.09
Assets ($)	—	.01	−.02	—	−.04	−.04	—	−.03	−.06
Competitive sector									
Manufacturing	.35	.49	.42	.38	.53	.55	−.03	−.01	.17
Mining	—	.11	.25	—	−.07	.29	—	−.07	.07
Agriculture	.04	—	.23	.01	—	.13	−.10	—	.11
White collar									
# White collar	—	.27	.25	—	.31	.38	—	−.04	.05
# Govt. employees	—	.54	.52	—	.54	.63	—	−.01	.31
Median education	.30	.34	.31	.28	.21	.30	−.16	−.19	−.12
Median income	.47	.07	.32	.44	.20	.48	−.18	−.17	−.09
Savings capital	—	.31	.62	—	.31	.74	—	−.05	.30
Demographic patterns									
Population size	.21	.18	.50	.21	.22	.61	—	−.02	.30
Population density	.42	.27	.21	.42	.51	.52	−.01	−.07	.03
Net migration	—	.45	.46	—	.29	.57	—	−.15	.23

In like manner, manufacturing exhibits a stronger association with each of the measures of task than does mining in 1960 and 1970. From 1950 to 1970 the manufacturing of the competitive sector emerges as a crucial variable of the bankruptcy court.

The association between pending cases and manufacturing is weak in 1950 ($r = .09$) but moderate by 1970 ($r = .39$). Pending cases measure the backlog of the court—those cases not resolved by the court in a given year; thus, it is a measure that indicates delay and congestion. By 1970, competitive-sector activity—particularly manufacturing—is associated with such cases, thus suggesting an important source of the court's problem. The significance of this factor is emphasized by contrast with the associations between manufacturing and filings, demand, asset cases, and business cases, which are moderate and rather stable from 1950 to 1970.

Consumer cases are not associated with measures of the competitive and monopoly sector. But, such cases are specific to consumer needs; therefore, it is to be expected that they are not correlated with more corporate-like measures. However, a large number of the tasks that come before the bankruptcy court are the result of consumer failure. What changes in the occupational structure might explain the significant growth in bankruptcies?

A "class is defined by men [and women] as they live their own history, and in the end, this is its only definition" (Thompson 1964, p. 11). A class must be examined as a social and cultural formation, rising from the historical processes of a period. A fraction of a class being subject to economic failure through bankruptcy must therefore be seen as a process in response to the formation and transformation of American society.

Bankruptcy is not a legal procedure used by the working class of the competitive sector (Jacob 1969; Shuchman 1971; Stanley et al., 1971). Those individuals who come to the bankruptcy court do so if and when they are unable to pay debts but will at the same time find this legal procedure advantageous in the long run. Competitive-sector employment is seasonal, unskilled, and often migratory. Therefore, the working class population that uses this court is drawn, primarily, from the state and monopoly sectors. But what changes specific to these sectors have caused an increase in the number of bankruptcies? Have there been changes in the occupational structure of the monopoly and state sectors that help to explain the increased demands on the court?

There are four considerations in approaching the sociology of stratification: occupation, class, status, and power (see, e.g., Bottomore 1964a, 1964b; Mills 1963; Weber 1946b). An occupation refers to a job that ideally yields a regular income, whereas class refers to a social group's relation to the means of production—the economic structure of a society. Focusing for the moment on the question of occupation, specific groups of occupations within the working class have declined in skill level due to the capitalist's need to continuously introduce labor-saving technologies. At the same time the expanding role of the state has made it the largest employer within the United States. The office was once

the site of mental labor and the shop the site of manual labor. . . . Insofar as this was true, the identification of office work with thinking and educated labor and of the production process proper with unthinking and uneducated labor, retained some validity. But once the office was itself subjected to the rationalization process, this contrast lost its force. (Braverman 1974, pp. 315–316)

Therefore, a white collar-blue collar distinction within the occupational structure does not any longer describe a relative skill or training level.

The most substantial proportional increase of occupations has taken place within categories of operatives, clerical workers, combined services, and the retail-sales sector (Braverman 1974; U.S. Bureau of the Census 1972). Thus, "the new mass working-class occupations tend to grow, not in contradiction to the speedy mechanization and 'automation' of industry, but in harmony with it" (Braverman 1974, p. 381). What in fact has taken place within this structure has been an expansion of the working class and a contraction of the middle class.

For example, from 1947 to 1958 the average American income rose by 50 percent; 32 percent of that rise was due to inflation, and 18 percent was an actual increase (Kolko 1962). Moreover, the income group that benefited primarily from this increase was the upper second and third income-tenth of the population, that is, managers and professionals.[8] It is these income groups that increasingly control the development of technologies within industry—that necessary innovative force that continually yields a surplus for the owners of capital (Baran and Sweezy 1966). Little, if any, relative increase in income has trickled down to the so-called skilled or semiskilled worker.

It is argued by others (Caplowitz 1974; Stanley et al. 1971) that the increasing consumer bankruptcy caseload is a result of the growth in an open-credit economy that has made money more accessible to the working population. This may in part be true. However, the increased rationalization within the work site as a result of the need constantly to decrease the labor time necessary to produce commodities, with its concomitant effects upon the working class (Edwards 1972; Gintis 1976), provides a more accurate starting point for understanding the growing demands on the bankruptcy court. The consumer bankrupt tends to be an individual of lower-middle-class income, high school education, married with children, and in a low-skill occupation (Jacob 1969; Stanley et al., 1971). As a group, the potential consumer bankrupt is locked into a low income bracket with little opportunity for upward mobility given the dynamics of the larger occupational structure.

In other words, the portion of the working class most likely to experience bankruptcy holds jobs in that portion of the occupational structure that has grown in greatest numbers since the post–World War II period. Tables 3-2 and

3-3 show zero-order correlations between measures of the white-collar sector and the tasks of the bankruptcy court in 1950, 1960, and 1970. The number of white-collar workers has a low to moderate association with most categories of bankruptcy cases; however, the relevance of this sector for the court is more profoundly exhibited by the effect of savings capital on most categories of bankruptcy cases. Savings capital measures the monies held by the public in savings-and-loan banks. The moderate to strong effect of this environmental variable by 1970 on most categories of cases emphasizes a point made earlier: bankruptcy is a legal procedure that affects the lower middle class, those with some money, not the very poor.

The state plays an increasingly important role in the economy. The occupational structure of the state sector complements and supports that of the monopoly sector; while the occupations in both are commonly referred to as white collar, the clerical skills demanded are increasingly rationalized and discrete categories of labor requiring less formal training. Tables 3–2 and 3–3 also show that the number of government employees exhibited a moderate to strong effect with most categories of bankruptcy cases. In fact, these associations suggest that the presence of government employees in a district—the state sector—may be a critical precondition for understanding the increase in bankruptcy cases.

In spite of these significant changes in the white-collar occupational structure, with its apparent effect upon this court, official indicators of education and income have continued to go up. To the extent that education is itself subject to the demands of a rationalized process of control, educators have produced a labor force with a higher median education (Bowles and Gintis 1976). Thus, the increased length of time in school from 10.6 years in 1948 to 12.4 years by 1970 indicates only that it now takes more time to pass on basic skills necessary for living in a consumptive, urbanized society (Braverman 1974). However, the rise in median education, given the shifts in the occupational structure, have not produced higher relative incomes for working individuals, whether they work in the private or the public sector. Median education and income are less exact measures of the white-collar sector; hence, education and income tend to exhibit a lower association with most types of bankruptcy cases.

The dynamics of industrialization, as they affect the number of units and earnings within manufacturing, mining, and agriculture, in conjunction with the merger activity of these economic sectors and their concomitant effect upon the white-collar occupational structure, are of primary importance in understanding the increase in the number of bankruptcy cases.

It is frequently argued that urban settings generate a more complex environment characterized in part by industrial growth, a more heterogeneous population, specialized services, and an increasing division of labor (Durkheim 1964; Wirth 1969; Warren 1967a, 1967b). The difference between "town" and "country" is symbolic of the modern mode of production—capitalism. Whereas the country (rural life) represents communal ties, small industry, exchange of products, and "natural instruments of production," the town represents human beings held together by exchange and dominated by money (Marx and Engels 1970, pp. 68–69). The town, the dominant structure of modern industrial life, is itself the result of a historical process.

The city becomes, in modern society, the center of "small scale manufacturing, retail trade, and food and other competitive sector services where productivity and wages are relatively low" (O'Connor 1973, p. 127). The city supplies the human resources, cheap labor power, for unskilled tasks; cities have the necessary resources to support a more precarious competitive sector.[9]

As Tables 3-2 and 3-3 show, population size, density (i.e., the median number of people per square mile per district), and net migration are moderately to strongly associated with various aspects of the court's task structure. Moreover, in most cases there is a significant increase from 1950 to 1970, suggesting that bankruptcy is more and more becoming an urban "institution." Thus, a fourth set of variables of the court's environment include the *demographic patterns* of a district.

It is clear that developments in the political economy of the court's environment have had a marked impact upon the size and complexity of demands of this organization. Yet, what of the relative importance of economic, social, and demographic variables? In order to answer this question, indicators of each of these sectors were selected to represent the nexus of processes that have shaped the activities—the caseload and casemix—of this court. Table 3-4 gives the results of the multiple and partial regression analysis, i.e., the separate (b^*) and joint (R^2) effects of these environmental factors on each category of bankruptcy filings.

The Caseload of the Bankruptcy Court: 1950 to 1970

The caseload of the court is described by pending cases, filings, and total demand. Each category of the caseload has increased markedly in the post-World War II period (see table 3-1a). In fact, by 1960 the total demand (192,300) on this court exceeded that of the early Depression years (124,200 in 1930). What economic, demographic, and social variables have been relatively the most essential in explaining this development?

Table 3-4 shows that the joint effects (R^2) of all five environmental variables and all categories of the court's caseload increased from 1950 to 1970. This means that the selected environmental indicators jointly "explain" the observed variances in a given category. For example, the joint effect of environmental variables explains 49 percent of the variance in pending cases by 1970; moreover, the change from 1950 $(R^2 = .02)$ to 1970 is most dramatic. Thus, in 1950 environmental factors did not explain the pending docket, whereas by 1970 environmental variables explained almost one-half of the variance in such cases. (Note, however, that data for government employees and mergers are not available for 1950.)

Table 3-4
Zero-Order Correlations (r), Standardized Partial Regression Coefficients (b*), and Squared Multiple Correlation Coefficients (R²) of Five Environmental Variables on Six Categories of Cases in the U.S. Bankruptcy Court in 1950, 1960, and 1970

		Pending cases			Filings			Demand			Asset cases			Business cases			Consumer cases		
		'50	'60	'70	'50	'60	'70	'50	'60	'70	'50	'60	'70	'50	'60	'70	'50	'60	'70
Merger	r	—	.40	.36	—	.49	.41	—	.47	.39	—	.46	.35	—	.81	.85	—	−.05	.09
	b*	—	.28	.08	—	.41	.11	—	.37	.10	—	.24	.04	—	.74	.72	—	—	−.04
Manufac.	r	.09	.41	.39	.41	.44	.44	.42	.45	.43	.35	.49	.42	.38	.53	.55	−.03	−.01	.17
	b*	.03	.19	.30	.44	.21	.40	.44	.21	.35	.20	.14	.35	.24	−.16	−.12	−.03	.06	.29
Govt. empl.	r	—	.43	.66	—	.43	.65	—	.45	.67	—	.54	.52	—	.54	.63	—	−.01	.31
	b*	—	.35	.59	—	.27	.56	—	.32	.59	—	.38	.42	—	.23	.36	—	.09	.31
Med. educ.	r	−.05	.13	.16	−.28	.19	.22	−.28	.17	.19	.30	.34	.31	.28	.21	.30	−.16	−.19	−.12
	b*	−.07	−.06	.02	−.29	—	.06	−.29	−.03	.04	.25	.15	.18	.24	−.02	.06	−.16	−.22	−.19
Pop. density	r	.13	.16	.20	.11	.16	.19	.13	.16	.20	.42	.27	.21	.42	.51	.52	−.01	−.07	.03
	b*	.13	−.32	−.25	−.05	−.36	−.34	−.03	−.36	−.30	.30	−.20	−.23	.28	.10	.09	.03	−.15	−.22
	R²	.02	.28	.49	.26	.35	.54	.26	.35	.53	.27	.39	.39	.28	.69	.84	.03	.05	.16

What of the separate, direct ($b*$) effect of each of these environmental variables on each category of the court's workload?

Pending Cases

The change in the direct effect of competitive sector manufacturing from 1950 ($b* = .03$) to 1970 ($b* = .30$) and government employees from 1960 ($b* = .35$) to 1970 ($b* = .59$) begins to isolate an important source of the congestion and delay in this court. That is, the changing structure of the competitive and state spheres discussed earlier has become the relevant factors in understanding the growth in the pending docket of this court.

By 1970 this court could be described as a backlogged organization; more specifically, it appears that growth in the number of state-sector workers along with the more precarious position of the competitive sector placed an increasing demand upon this court in the twenty years under examination. The organizational structure of the bankruptcy court seems to be increasingly unable to process cases within a reasonable period of time: changes within the court's environment have not been in harmony with changes within the court's organization; however, the possibility of introducing a "more or less incomplete" reform to "solve" this problem remains a political question.

Both the large absolute increase in pending cases shown in table 3-1a and the analysis shown in table 3-4 empirically suggest that the organizational structure of a collegial organization such as this court may be inadequate for the tasks presented.

The question then arises: is the backlog of the court a "qualitative" problem as well? Is the backlog of the court problematic for lawyers, trustees, creditors, and consumers in such a way that the court is ineffective for them? Moreover, what may be a problem that must be solved for creditors or consumers, in this case backlog, may not be a problem for lawyers. Thus, change in the structure of the court to solve the problem of backlog depends upon factors other than just the court's documented inefficiency.

Filings

The competitive sector as measured by manufacturing has had a rather stable simple (r) effect and direct ($b*$) effect on filings from 1950 to 1970. By contrast, the tension between the monopoly (i.e., mergers) and state (i.e., government employees) sectors from 1960 to 1970 seems to have been the critical factor in the rise in bankruptcy filings. Whereas the number of mergers per district had a decreasing direct effect from 1960 ($b* = .41$) to 1970 ($b* = .11$), the number of government employees had a greater direct effect from 1960

(b^* = .27) to 1970 (b^* = .56). Finally, by 1970 the number of government employees was the main factor in explaining the joint effect (R^2 = .54) of bankruptcy filings.

Most bankruptcy cases remain straight procedures; bankruptcies where there is little money or assets to distribute (see tables 3-1a and 3-1b). Thus, most bankruptcies are "consumer" cases. The findings from table 3-4 suggest that the workers of the growing state sector are, however, the important factor in an explanation of the court's workload.

Demand

The standardized regression coefficients (b^*) of each of the court's environmental variables on total demand essentially support the results of the previous discussion. That is, by 1970 the presence of government employees (b^* =.59) in a district is the primary factor in an explanation of demand (R^2 = .53).

That the state sector is the primary variable in an explanation of pending cases, filings, and demand is not surprising since the government is the largest employer of white-collar, clerical workers in the United States, workers who enjoy "safe" employment—i.e., civil-service protection—but apparently with little economic security. The state must, given the constraints of monopoly capitalism, continue to employ those workers who the "private" sector can no longer support (Baran and Sweezy 1966; Gordon 1972; O'Connor 1973). However the state like the monopoly sector must also constantly introduce technological innovations; hence, there is a growth in "mass occupations" in the state sector as well. Ironically then, the bankruptcy court appears to be a protector of the workers for other branches of the state.

A traditional role of the state is to preserve social "harmony" between potential "factions" (O'Connor 1973; but also see Bowles and Gintis 1975; Pivan and Cloward 1971; Hamilton 1961; Kolko 1976; Williams 1961). To that end, the federal budget is, in part, described by various "social expenses"— projects and services that are introduced to mitigate social conflicts. The best example of social expense allocation is of course welfare, which is seen to control economic and social problems resulting from high unemployment in an advanced capitalist society (Pivan and Cloward 1971). However, the state's expenditure on the organization of the bankruptcy court is also a social expense to control growing economic insecurity of its own work force.

The Casemix of the Bankruptcy Court: 1950 to 1970

Table 3-4 shows the separate, direct (b^*) and joint (R^2) effects of environmental variables with asset cases, business cases, and consumer cases—those bankruptcy proceedings that tend to be more complex legal procedures. What has been the relative effect of economic, social, and demographic variables on these categories of cases from 1950 to 1970?

Asset Cases

Asset cases may be either corporate or consumer procedures; moreover, the definition of an asset case varies from state to state since exempt properties are presently determined by the state, not by federal statute. An asset case, however, is one in which some monies are available for payment to creditors.

In spite of this lack of uniformity in the definition of such procedures, the rising number of asset cases are in part explained by the nexus of environmental factors that describe this court. Thus, the joint effect of environmental factors accounts for over one-third of the variance in asset cases in 1960 (R^2 = .39) and 1970 (R^2 = .39). This suggests that state differences, as they affect asset cases, may be outweighed by structural developments in the court's environment.

This point is supported also by the standardized regression coefficients shown in table 3-4. In 1960, the number of government employees was the main factor (b^* = .38) in accounting for the joint effect of such cases. However, in 1970 the direct effect of both manufacturing (b^* = .35) and government employees (b^* = .42) was moderate. By 1970, the competitive sector along with the white-collar workers of the state sector accounted for the asset cases of this court. The moderate effect of government employees in 1960 and 1970 supports the fact that the definition of such cases is not uniform from state to state and hence may affect such workers differently. However, the moderate direct effect of competitive-sector manufacturing by 1970 suggests that the court has been hearing more cases with a larger proportionate share of "real" money for disbursement among creditors since such cases are, in part, accounted for by competitive-sector industries. But in either case, the possibility of disbursing monies to creditors creates work for the personnel of the court, particularly when one realizes that the amount in question is often minimal and yet must be "equitably" divided among numerous creditors.

Business Cases

The number of corporate reorganization procedures has remained rather stable from 1950 to 1970 (see table 3-1b). Yet the joint effect of environmental variables increased dramatically from 1950 (R^2 = .28) to 1970 (R^2 = .84). (Note that data on mergers and government employees are not available for 1950; however, the joint effect also increases from 1960 (R^2 = .69) to 1970 and is based upon exactly comparable variables.) That is, by 1970 environmental factors explain over three-fourths of the variance in business cases.

Moreover, the results of the multiple regression analysis essentially confirm the earlier discussion of business cases (table 3-3). That is, in both 1960 (b^* = .74) and 1970 (b^* = .72) the merger activity of the monopoly sector is the primary variable in an explanation of such cases. Moreover, business cases are the only category of bankruptcy proceeding in which monopoly-sector activity emerges as the critical factor.

While the actual reorganization cases that come before this court may be small scale, competitive businesses (i.e., manufacturing: in 1950 r = .38; in 1960 r = .53; in 1970 r = .55), they tend, nevertheless, to be explained by merger within the monopoly sector. In spite of the fact that monopoly industries often rely upon smaller businesses for innovative ideas (Baran and Sweezy 1966) and for other trade and market outlets, these findings suggest that it is increasingly difficult for such businesses to actually survive.

Business cases are a very small share of the court's workload; as compared to other types of cases they are, however, the product of a distinct set of factors. This suggests that the task structure of the court may be differentiated by demands generated from consumers on the one hand and businesses on the other. With the prospect of reform, the court seems to be serving two distinct groups that possibly present two distinct sets of demands.

Though the bankruptcy court is one organization in its formal structure, this analysis suggests that there may be two informal organizations (Blau and Scott 1962; *House Hearings* 1976, pp. 1142-87). If this is true, then representatives of consumer and business interests will be drawn from very different parts of the legal community and should take opposite positions on the proposed reform of the court. However, the interests of both of these groups cannot be advocated directly. Consumer or business groups that may go bankrupt are not likely to take form around a question of change in the structure of the court. While businesses and consumers share the need of relying upon others (i.e., consumer groups, lawyers, creditors, judges, etc.) to speak for them, the resources and organization of these groups may give some, particularly consumer groups, a notably disadvantageous bargaining position.

Consumer Cases

Consumer reorganization procedures are perhaps the most controversial bankruptcy option (Shuchman 1971). At all three points in time, environmental variables do not, to any significant degree, explain the rise in the number of such cases. This is in rather marked contrast to all other categories of cases.

Hence, these findings suggest that consumer reorganization procedures are explained by factors other than the demands of the court's environment. Consumers who initiate bankruptcy have the option, usually, of selecting either a straight procedure or a Chapter XIII procedure. The findings here suggest that choosing Chapter XIII proceedings may have more to do with the inclination and policy aspects of legal and judicial decision making in a particular court than with the processes and relations of the court's environment. That is, the number of consumer cases in a district cannot be monitored by the judges of a court; however, a judge or lawyer may choose effectively to persuade an individual to pursue a particular bankruptcy procedure once the case is in court.[10]

How then do these tasks of the court become political points of controversy in the process of reform?

The Politics of the Court's Caseload and Casemix

The development of laws and organizations to administer such laws is mediated by the demands of the state apparatus, the market, and the needs of dominant strata. Weber (1954) argues that to the extent that the law remains a viable instrument to regulate the affairs of society it must in essence become a more rational, rule-like body of knowledge. That is, the law itself is subject to processes of transformation.

Reform is a *political* process. In that process interest groups may describe each of the features of the task structure (i.e., demand, complexity, etc.) as a strategy to maintain a collegial structure; or conversely, others may define the task structure to support the establishment of a bureaucratic organization. That is, the content of the work of the court, the body of law, does not, by definition, suggest a unilinear evolution. The definition of the size and complexity of the task structure by various interest groups is itself open to qualitative interpretation. However, the task structure will ultimately be controlled by those strata that are able to direct the transformation of the court. Hence, the direction of reform is a political question and not a predetermined process.

At this point, the issues are specified by groups. With the possible exception of the judges, various interest groups speak to specific aspects of the court's task structure. For example, representatives of organized labor speak to the issue of redefining wages; creditors speak primarily to the issue of exemptions whereas attorneys are concerned with business bankruptcies.[11] The groups who address various aspects of this issue include judges, creditors and bankers, consumer law advocates, representatives of organized labor, practicing attorneys, and legal scholars. We will first consider the judge's position, and then address a selection of the more representative issues covered by each of the others.

Judges. The judges begin by suggesting that the Commission's work has been far better in its substantive recommendations than in its structural recommendations: "The Commission performed far better, in our view, in its proposals for substantive improvements in consumer bankruptcy laws than it did in those affecting the administration of those proceedings. This, we believe, once again, is due to the difference in background and experience between their views and our own" (*Senate Hearings* 1975, p. 58). According to the judges, judges in bankruptcy have superior knowledge in the area due to their day-to-day experience with the law: their "pragmatic" knowledge is a legitimating tool for their position. Thus, they can argue that "consumer cases . . . are not miniature bankruptcy business cases. The fact that they deal with human beings indicates the importance that we apply legal standards and procedures which reflect the radically different origins of consumer insolvency problems and that we recognize the humanity of its primary victims" (*Senate Hearings* 1975, p. 49; also see *House Hearings* 1976, pp. 1315-32). If one cannot make generalizations about consumer cases, as the judges suggest, then one cannot make rules about how such procedures should be executed (see, e.g., *House Hearings* 1976, pp. 1278-1307). And by implication, if one cannot make formal guidelines, then it is necessary for a judge, rather than a civil servant, to decide such cases.

The Constitution does not distinguish between consumer and business debtors. Therefore, the judges argue that the reform of this court cannot take steps to make such an arbitrary distinction: "All legal questions within the purview of the new Bankruptcy Act belong in the same bankruptcy court whether they emanate from a consumer case, a business liquidation, or a relief proceeding. It is important to avoid the appearance as well as the fact of any elitism in the court's availability to litigants" (*House Hearings* 1975, p. 517). Thus, the judges argue that the establishment of separate organizations, as suggested by the Commission, implicitly establishes an elite structure—a court—for businesses and a mass structure—an agency—for consumers.

The establishment of a court that is coequal with the district court structure implies some changes in the tasks for this new court. Thus, the judges argue that not only should both consumer and business cases remain under the auspices of the court, but railroad reorganization cases should also be added to the responsibilities of the bankruptcy judges. The judges argue that such cases clearly fall within the domain of this court's activities; moreover, the addition of railroad cases would significantly improve the prestige of this court (*House Hearings* 1975, pp. 583-90; *House Hearings* 1976, pp. 2594-2614). And the judges argue that improved status of the court would benefit both consumer and business clients. Moreover, there are practicing attorneys who directly support the judges on this issue (*House Hearings* 1976, p. 2517).[12]

In summary, the judges view the division of the court's tasks along the lines proposed by the Commission as a violation of Constitutional guidelines that guarantee a forum for the litigation of all such cases. Moreover, the

"shy, reticent and uneducated" consumer debtors who appear before our bankruptcy courts each year should not be relegated to undifferentiating, "revolving door" treatment by personnel of a bureaucracy bereft of the flexibility and immediacy with which to address the inexhaustible circumstantial variations which are invariably posed in the course of extended consumer insolvency proceedings. (Cyr 1975, pp. 129–30; also reprinted in *Senate Hearings* 1975)

Creditors and Bankers. In discussing the redefinition of this court's tasks, creditors and bankers are concerned with specific issues: for example, whether exemptions should be established by states or by the federal government, and what dischargeability of properties should include.

Exemption Laws. Exemption Laws refer to guidelines that define which properties are outside the purview of bankruptcy litigation. Such exemption laws are presently defined by each state and, as a result, vary considerably (Vukowich 1974). Though the Congress has the authority to define a uniform bankruptcy law, it does not presently have the authority to control exemption standards. The Commission's Bill suggests that exemption laws be made uniform under federal guidelines. Again, this suggestion by the Commission reflects a move to establish a formally defined and codified statement that complements an administrative as opposed to an adjudicatory organization.

The consumer creditors support the Commission's Bill concerning the issue of exemptions (*Senate Hearings* 1975, p. 537). They argue that a uniform code of exemptions would prevent "shopping" for a bankruptcy forum where the state might give the client a better chance. In those states where there are very few exemptions allowed, a uniform code would raise the standards of truly facilitating a fresh start for the bankrupt client. However, business creditors tend to argue that exemption guidelines should remain under state jurisdiction (*Senate Hearings* 1975, pp. 427–53). This difference in position between consumer and business creditors also characterizes other issues of court reform, a point that we will return to in later chapters.

Bankers' representatives suggest also that a uniform code of exemptions will not be seen favorably by the respective states. It is not possible, they argue, to suggest a uniform code that would meet the approval of the many states. However, they go on to argue that they also have no suggestion as to what a meaningful baseline might entail (*Senate Hearings* 1975, pp. 135–36; also see *House Hearings* 1976, pp. 1021–28). Thus, these two groups, bankers and creditors, support different positions regarding the degree to which exemption laws should be changed under the rubric of bankruptcy reform.[13]

Dischargeability. The Commission's Bill has sought to establish that debts incurred as a result of an inaccurate financial statement filed by the consumer with a credit agency or bank should be discharged from payment if bankruptcy results. It is the argument of the Commission that it is the responsibility of those granting loans to assess accurately the financial status of the individual.

Clearly, such a reform is not in the best interest of creditors; thus creditors support the Judges' Bill when they argue that "if a debtor is not accountable for the financial statement he is being given a civil license to commit fraud. Why make bankruptcy more attractive, accessible and protective for every debtor who doesn't want to pay his bills? The relief should be restricted to honest debtors who are unable to pay their bill" (*Senate Hearings*, 1975, p. 190; also see *House Hearings* 1976, pp. 897–907, 1332–34). Part of a creditor's procedure includes the investigation of a client's financial status. The creditors argue that if that step is taken, the court must guarantee the creditor a fair and equitable opportunity to recover lost monies (*Senate Hearings* 1975, p. 188; also see *House Hearings* 1976, p. 1047). Moreover, the creditors argue that other bills have been passed by Congress, in particular the Consumer Credit Protection Act, which seek to correct problems in the area of consumer lending. They conclude, therefore, that this is not a question that should be addressed at this time (*Senate Hearings* 1975, p. 174). The existing specialization of the law gives creditors the leverage to argue that such issues are not to be addressed in this arena, in spite of their direct relevance to the legal guidelines of bankruptcy.

Implicit in the creditors' argument is the assumption that the honesty of debtors is a question prior to a court hearing. The Commission's Bill is seen to take the "easy way out" insofar as it argues that it is difficult to determine the honesty of debtors. In summary, the creditors state that they "do not subscribe to the belief that the time has come to enact laws abridging the freedom of contract under the guise of necessary social legislation" (*Senate Hearings* 1975, p. 142).

U.S. Attorney's Office. The representatives of the U.S. Attorney's Office are opposed to the expansion of the jurisdiction of the bankruptcy court as proposed by the judges, and suggest that railroad reorganization cases should remain within the domain of the district court (*Senate Hearings* 1975, p. 481; also see *House Hearings* 1976, p. 2098). In keeping with their general support of a more codified and formal approach to bankruptcy, they also support the establishment of a uniform exemption code as suggested by the Commission.[14]

Practicing Attorneys. Chapters X and XI are different legal options for the reorganization of business enterprises (see page 36). In a word, Chapter XI was intended for the reorganization of smaller businesses, but through the decades the owners of larger corporations have come to rely upon this bankruptcy option. Not surprisingly, the future of these legal options comes into debate since the judges and Commission suggest alternative solutions. Whereas the Commission proposes that these legal options be consolidated into one chapter (VII) of the Bankruptcy Code, the Judges' Bill proposes a maintenance of the status quo, that is, that Chapters X and XI remain distinct legal options.

Practicing attorneys in the area of bankruptcy set the tone for this debate when they argue,

How two chapters which are "legally, mutually exclusive paths to attempted financial rehabilitation" with disparate needs, can be merged into one, adopting the strict standard of reorganization wholly unsuited to the composition standard, is hard to conceive. The Commission seems to have succumbed to theory and forgotten that experience makes the chapters work. (*Senate Hearings* 1975, p. 395)

Other attorneys have taken a similar position (see, e.g., *Senate Hearings* 1975, pp. 552-77; *House Hearings* 1976, pp. 1651-60). In essence, attorneys who have practiced before this court are familiar with the present arrangement but attempt to rest their case on the argument that "Chapter X and XI have served the business economy well and should [therefore] continue as separate chapters" (*Senate Hearings* 1975, p. 402).

Of course, the judges themselves make a case for their position and provide further material for this question (*House Hearings* 1976, p. 1903). Since business creditors play an important role in reorganization procedures, they also take a position in support of the Judges' Bill (*House Hearings* 1976, p. 2499).

But this is only one side of the picture. For there are those practicing attorneys who support the consolidation of these business reorganization procedures. Consolidation, uniformity, and rationality also support, as Weber argues, the liberal ideology of equality and due process. Hence, it is not surprising that those attorneys in support of change, that is, consolidation, echo this truism: "What a consolidated chapter essentially does is to provide a *democratization of the proceedings*. There is more creditor participation and there is more creditor ability to get the best possible reorganization plan for the distressed business entity, and thereby create a viable business concern." (*House Hearings* 1976, p. 1899; emphasis added).

There are other supporters of consolidation, especially legal scholars (*Senate Hearings* 1975, pp. 981-1006). One legal scholar argues that "the people who are opposing the idea at this point are simply people who do not want to change their method of practing law " (*Senate Hearings* 1975, p. 994). Finally, the American Bar Association supports consolidation (*Senate Hearings* 1975, p. 994).

Why this difference of opinion by those who practice before this court and hence these differences in affiliated group support? The position of the ABA provides an interesting clue to this question. Consolidation reflects the general ethos of the Commission's Bill with its emphasis upon the rationalization of this institution; it complements the possibility of initiating even corporate reorganization cases in an administrative agency, thus reserving the courtroom for only "controversial" cases. But as we showed in the first chapter of this book, such a "reform" in fact supports business interests. Thus, the ABA's position on this aspect of reform seems to support the economic and political interest of its wealthier constituency. By contrast, those who support the Judges' Bill may be lawyers for "family" businesses; that is, their livelihood revolves around the representation of that group where the distinction between consumer and business bankruptcies is, at best, unclear. The difference of opinion among various groups of practicing attorneys reflects the larger stratification of the legal profession itself, a point we will return to in chapter 4.

Organized Labor. The representatives of organized labor introduce yet another dimension into the redefinition of the court's tasks. They are concerned with a very specific aspect of the Bankruptcy Code (see, e.g., McConnell 1966). They have three basic concerns. First, as the present law states, a trustee in a bankruptcy case need not honor a labor contract. Neither bill, according to labor representatives, adequately addresses this issue. Second, the definition of wage is out-of-step with contemporary trends. Pensions and insurance policies negotiated between employer and employee should be incorporated into a legal definition of wage. And finally, the Bankruptcy Code should expand the period of wage priority to employers from six months to one year. The representatives of labor are concerned with those aspects of bankruptcy procedure that have to do with corporate bankruptcy and reorganization and its attendant effects upon workers.

If a business client enters the bankruptcy court, that court must seek to protect the employees of such businesses: "Even if the collective bargaining agreement could be abrogated unilaterally, the trustee, as the employer, would still be obligated to bargain with the union under basic requirements of the National Labor Relations Act, and could still make no changes in wage or working conditions without first bargaining with the union." (*Senate Hearings* 1975, p. 278)

Labor representatives argue that the law does not suggest that trustees have the right or authority to ignore contracts with employees. They believe that in a time when the dockets of the court are increasingly plagued by corporate cases, it is the responsibility of the court to protect the needs of workers.

In previous Supreme Court decisions, the definition of wage (i.e., excluding insurance or pension) has been upheld by the Court with the suggestion that Congress amend the term (*Senate Hearings* 1975, p. 316). Given this suggestion by the Court, it is labor's position that the reform of bankruptcy provides the opportunity to do exactly that.

Finally, the representatives of organized labor seek to guarantee wages to employees for a longer period of time. Wages must be made a priority by this court when corporate bankruptcy ensues if the court is to serve as a forum which equally protects all parties (also see *House Hearings* 1976, pp. 2426–53).

Earlier findings showed that the indicators of the court's environment were increasingly associated with consumer bankruptcies: those of the expanding white-collar working population—clericals, operatives, sales and service personnel—those whose occupations are increasingly represented through labor unions. Thus, it is important to note that spokespersons of organized labor represent only those workers on one issue, that of the possibility of corporate bankruptcy. However, such workers are, in fact, potential consumer bankrupts. The leadership within labor unions is more in touch with its negotiator—the employer—than the source of its own representation—the employee. In other words, labor's bargaining position before Congress does not take into account the fact that, in part, it represents perhaps the largest single source of work for this court—consumer bankruptcies.[15]

Consumer Groups. Consumer law advocates argue (unlike any other group) that the heart of the reform must be changes in the statutes, which would redefine the tasks of this court. But consumer advocates basically criticize both proposals:

The choice before this Committee of the proper forum for bankruptcy ought to be made on the basis of the greatest likelihood for genuine reform. The National Consumer Law Center is not satisfied that either proposal is inherently better than the other. The problem is one of building proper safeguards into the statute so as to require that the forum be responsive to relief as they arise. (*Senate Hearings* 1975, p. 316)

In their view, the Commission's Bill degrades and works against the needs of consumers by relegating their case to an administrative agency.

Consumer law advocates go on to argue that the problem of consumer cases must be considered an absolutely separate issue from that of business cases. If this step is taken, then, and only then, will it be possible to compose a set of laws that fairly serve the interests of consumers. Thus, consumer law advocates support neither proposal but, unlike representatives of labor, they do not present a well-defined alternative that might be debated and possibly incorporated into the final bill. Without presenting such a concrete set of alternatives, it is hard to imagine that the criticisms of this group will have an impact.

In essence, consumer law advocates abdicate their role of cultivating a meaningful alternative for consumer bankruptcy cases. In this vacuum, legal scholars state the needs of the consumer and the changes that are necessary.

Legal Scholars. Legal scholars support the establishment of an equitable bankruptcy court by taking a "moral" position. The question of morality surrounds bankruptcy, both pro and con. In a society dominated by an open-credit economy, the legal scholar insists, it is morally necessary to provide a forum for the handling of consumer cases:

The vast majority of our bankrupts are the victims of a credit economy with which they cannot cope, just as the vast majority of our motor accident victims are the necessary byproduct of a system of transportation with which they cannot cope. In the one sense, as in the other, it seems eminently more human and sensible to provide them relief, at some cost to the government but mostly at the cost of other users of the system, than to run around passing moral judgments. (*House Hearings* 1975, p. 342; also see *House Hearings* 1976, pp. 1410–24)

Thus, legal scholars further legitimate consumer bankruptcy as a viable and acceptable procedure.

Conclusion: The Rationalization of Adjudication

Judges are the only group in the process of bankruptcy court reform who address the overall implications of a redefinition of the court's tasks. The scope of their presentation of this issue is significant. It suggests that those interest groups most directly affected by court reform cannot ignore any aspect of possible change if they are to maintain control over the organization of bankruptcy in the future. The more specific issues addressed by other groups (i.e., creditors, labor, U.S. Attorney) also raise an important point. Support of reform in a particular direction may not entail a unidimensional position.

The rise of lawyers complements the needs of a capitalistic system: "Legal training has primarily been in the hands of lawyers from among whom also the judges are recruited, i.e., in the hands of a group which is active in the service of the propertied class, and particularly capitalistic, private interest and which has to gain its livelihood from them" (Weber 1954, p. 318). The control over knowledge by a group of legal experts has itself contributed to the codification and rationalization of the law into subfields of expertise. As the "experts," in this case the lawyers and judges, are in debt to the mechanisms of a market and a propertied class, they must cooperate with those forces in order to survive as viable actors on the historical stage. In spite of "the use of jurors and similar lay judges [they] will not suffice to stop the continuous growth of the technical element in the law and hence its character as a specialist's domain" (Weber 1954, p. 321).[16]

Traditionally, American courts of law can be described as "law-finding" organizations.[17] Presented with a dispute, the judge, as arbitrator and spokesperson for the court, "finds" previous law that is relevant to the case at hand.[18] However, the activities of a market, coupled with the rise of a bourgeoisie, have set the historical stage for the rationalizing processes of law, for the systematic creation of law; in the U.S. this is seen in the rise of administrative law.

The demands of a market economy require control over its processes, and these processes rest upon rules, calculation, and predictability. In Weber's terms, central to this process is the need for legitimation of the contract as a negotiable instrument (also see Durkheim 1964; Renner 1949). Therefore, the traditional function of law is mediated by the demands of the market of a capitalist society:

The present day significance of contract is primarily the result of the high degree to which our economic system is market-oriented and the role played by money. The increased importance of the private law contract in general is thus the legal reflex of the market orientation of our economy. . . . In accordance with this fundamental transformation of the general character of the voluntary agreement we shall call the more primitive type "status contract" and that which is peculiar to the exchange or market economy "purposive contract." (Weber 1954, p. 105)

The theme here reflects the primary thrust of Weber's work on law in particular and on modern domination in general. As the market takes on more significant dimensions, human conduct comes to be oriented toward purposive, i.e., rational, ends, whereas the voluntary contract of traditional society, where legitimation comes from the "eternal past, in the rightness and appropriateness of the traditional way of doing things" (Mouzelis 1972, p. 16), rests upon a status position that is inherited rather than achieved. Western civilization is distinct from other social formations because of the centrality of the market as a rationalizing force on the law.[19] As Gerth and Mills suggest,

the more he [Weber] approaches modern industrial capitalism, the more willing is he to see capitalism as a pervasive and unifying affair. High capitalism absorbs other institutions into its own image, and numerous institutional criss-crosses give way to a set of parallel forces heading in the same direction. This direction is toward the rationalization of all spheres of life (1946, p. 66).[20]

Or as Weber puts it, "any legal guarantee is directly at the service of economic interest to a very large extent" (1954, p. 37). While Weber's analysis of law should not be confused with a Marxian class analysis, his work does recurrently suggest that the law importantly serves economic interests. However, unlike Marx, Weber argues that at the core of the state are individuals who with their staffs have a "monopoly of the legitimate use of force" (Wright 1974). The chief of a state may be part of a group or a stratum, but never of a class.

The history of Anglo-American law demonstrates that capitalism can develop without formal-rational procedures as part of its legal tradition. However, the rise of lawyers as experts and therefore as protectors of their domain of knowledge, coupled with the centrality of the market economy and the demands for calculability and rationality that it poses, seem to make it inevitable that a more rational legal procedure will succeed, and come to dominate what may have been an adversarial process resting upon the interpretation of individual cases.

For each of these themes there are political and historical factors that are unique to the bankruptcy court. Thus on the one hand, Weber's work provides guideposts for analysis of the organizational formation and transformation within this court. But on the other hand, the analysis of a particular case, the bankruptcy court, may circumscribe and delimit the degree to which legal change is inevitably rational.

Notes

1. The budget of a court as well as the addition of judge slots are decided by the legislative branch which thus directly limits the control of judges over their work.

2. Of course a general consideration in this research is the degree to which law can become specialized or formalized and still require judges and a court structure to decide cases. This point will be reconsidered later.

3. While both Chapter X and XI cases refer to reorganization proceedings, there are three basic areas of difference between the two: control of the proceeding, regulation of creditors and their representation, and the nature of the plan of rearrangement (*Report of the Commission on Bankruptcy Laws* 1973). In a Chapter XI proceeding, control of the plan of rearrangement is with the debtor who initiates the procedures. There are no controls over the representation of creditors and there must be an investigation of the viability of liquidation for the benefit of creditors prior to commencement of a rearrangement proceeding. In a Chapter X case, the judge appoints an independent trustee who runs the business. The trustee has broad powers over the business and initiates the plan of payment. In a Chapter X case, the nature of creditor representation must be fully clarified within the court, and senior creditor interests are given priority over those of junior creditors. As originally conceived, Chapter XI procedures were intended for smaller, closely controlled corporations; however, Chapter XI has "evolved into the dominant reorganization vehicle and very substantial debtors are able to reorganize in Chapter XI" (*Report* 1973, p. 265). Chapter XII procedures also refer to rearrangements; however, this reference is to a particular situation that developed in Illinois and is rarely, if ever, used.

4. This latter consideration must be distinguished from the above point. That is, this is not an economic analysis of bankruptcy itself where fluctuations in the relations of the economy affect the number of bankruptcies per se (see Gort 1962). Rather this is an examination of an organization, the bankruptcy court, whose primary tasks are generated by changes in industrial patterns. To that end, I have selected economic and social variables that will help to explain a primary source of pressure on the organization of the court. In this light, this analysis should be considered as part of a larger tradition where the perspective of the sociological question is used as a tool to understand the social relations and dynamics of a research site, be it in medicine, law, social welfare, etc. In the case of this particular organization, one of the primary dimensions is the impact of industrial change.

5. The underlying theme of classical economic analysis (that of Ricardo and Smith) is the independence of the economic sector from the political and social sectors. The formation of distinct economic spheres encompasses all elements of industry: land, labor, and money (Polanyi 1972). Not only is land a commodity for sale, but human labor power and money themselves become objects of

exchange. To the extent that labor and money become commodities, the structure of social relations between human beings is altered in a fundamental manner: "Capitalist production had its historical root precisely in the transformation of human productive activity itself into a commodity" (Dobb 1972, p. 54). Insofar as production rests upon the sale of human labor power, existence of this form of exchange relies upon a class structure in which one class has the power to buy the labor power of another class. That class that owns capital in sufficient amounts to purchase labor power and to buy the raw material necessary for production is, in the broadest sense, a capitalist class. "In terms of the labor time expended in production in relation to the labor time that the capitalist can command as a result of the sale of the community, this [production] is called surplus value. In terms of money itself, this is called profit" (O'Connor 1974, p. 60). A fundamental dynamic of the capitalist system is the need to produce and realize surplus value. Thus, the capitalist has two objectives: to produce value that has value in exchange—commodities, and to produce a commodity that has value greater than the sum of the value used to produce it (Marx 1967). As the capitalist enterprise has become more developed, the tactics taken to maintain this balance have become increasingly complex. However, these fundamental dynamics remain the formation within which the capitalist enterprise must operate. Given this position, the separation of management from ownership has not fundamentally altered this need for capitalist expansion. In support of this position is the work of Baran and Sweezy (1966), Mattick (1969), and O'Connor (1973). For a counter-argument, see Dahrendorf (1959).

6. As an aside, while the competitive sector of the economy is less critical for the overall economic strength of the United States, the executive has been forced to play an increasingly central role in the control of this sector's labor force: "In the past, the main domestic problem was the relationship between monopoly capital and organized labor. Today, the executive is more and more preoccupied with the conditions of unorganized labor in the competitive sector, particularly black and other minority workers condemned by racism to the competitive sector and to poorly paid jobs in the monopoly sector" (O'Connor 1973, p. 82; also see Gordon 1972).

7. See Appendix C for a further discussion of these variables.

8. Collecting data on income distribution has been done in many different ways by various governmental (i.e., U.S. Bureau of the Census and the Office of Business Economics of the Department of Commerce) and nongovernmental (e.g., National Industrial Conference Board and Survey Research Center) agencies. Differences revolve around both the definition of the income unit and the number of income groups within the total population. Kolko suggests that the most accurate results are obtained if the total population is divided into income tenths, as has been done by the National Industrial Conference Board. For a further discussion of this problem, see Gabriel Kolko, *Wealth and Power in America* (1962).

9. As O'Connor (1973) points out, the city-suburb relationship is in many ways a mechanism of impoverishment of one-third of the working class. Furthermore, as the city comes to symbolize and dominate the competitive sector, which rests upon a labor force of blacks, Puerto Ricans, and other minority groups, it simultaneously demands the contradictory input of social consumption capital—capital that goes to the poor as a stopgap mechanism.

10. This is not unlike plea bargaining in criminal law where the police, prosecution, and judge effectively persuade most offenders to plead guilty and thus avoid a trial. (See Blumberg 1970; Garfinkel 1956; Heydebrand and Seron, forthcoming).

11. But these are only three among many issues that are in fact debated. The topics were selected for the range of opinion they generated and the scope of their effect on the larger society. Therefore, such topics as municipal bankruptcies were omitted from this discussion. See Appendix B for a further discussion of this point.

12. The Interstate Commerce Commission (ICC) testified concerning this question of railroad reorganization since they have been historically involved in these cases. Basically, it is the position of representatives of the ICC that both bills are problematic since they stress "judicialization," though in different courts. They conclude that "it is important to eliminate some of the duplication of functions between the courts and the ICC. But we propose accomplishing this by giving the ICC the primary role in transportation and procedural aspects of rail reorganization while giving the courts essentially review functions" (*House Hearings* 1976, p. 2585). This is the only area in which the representatives of the ICC played an active role in the debates on reform.

13. While the issue of exemptions directly affects creditors, other important interest groups lend support. For example, practicing attorneys support business interests when they make a case for maintaining state control over exemptions (*House Hearings* 1976, p. 1256), though others do support a uniform code (*House Hearings* 1976, p. 1539). Legal scholars generally support a move toward uniformity, i.e., rationality (see e.g., *House Hearings* 1976, p. 864).

14. The representatives of the Department of Justice also testified on some more esoteric aspects of bankruptcy; this included testimony on municipal defaults, especially of New York City (*House Hearings* 1976, pp. 716-31), and on taxes (*House Hearings* 1976, pp. 2000-2034; also see *Senate Hearings* 1975, pp. 781-89).

15. O'Connor (1973) argues that the competitive sector is characterized by unorganized, unskilled labor and that the monopoly and state sectors are characterized by organized and skilled labor. Organized labor represents the ILGWU, the AFL-CIO, the United Auto Workers, and the Amalgamated Clothing Workers of America. O'Connor's categorization of nonunion-union as one distinguishing characteristic of monopoly-state sector and competitive sector breaks down when one realizes that the clothing industry is primarily a competitive-sector

industry with an organized labor force (ILGWU and Amalgamated Clothing Workers of America). However, the AFL-CIO and the United Auto Workers epitomize the role of organized labor within an emerging "social-industrial complex;" both unions have maintained a hegemonic position over rank and file workers and influenced the direction of state-sector spending. Though O'Connor's distinction is not completely accurate when one considers the broad spectrum of organized labor, the stance taken by the representatives of labor in this debate does reflect a position that complements organized labor's relationship to the state and monopoly sectors and clearly suggests that the stronger unions (i.e., the AFL–CIO and the United Auto Workers) give cues to less powerful unions when relevant political issues arise.

16. As a technique for maintaining control over adjudication, lawyers in England controlled the training of other lawyers through a guild system: "They retained in their hands juristic training as an empirical and highly developed technology, and they successfully fought all moves toward rational law that threatened their social and material position" (Weber 1946a, p. 217).

17. As Weber points out, the law can be either "found" or "made." "Law-finding" denotes that the law that is decreed is believed to exist, that it is found rather than enacted. "Law-making" is the process whereby human beings, as part of their human activities, create laws which, in turn, further define a legitimate order. Law making and law finding can exist simultaneously or in isolation. Weber begins his analysis of law as an outgrowth of his questions concerning the normative beliefs that define social conduct, or the expectations of conduct, between people or groups of people. In this sense, Weber's work on law draws upon his assumptions about the sociological question, or how human activities are oriented. A "legitimate order," or set of shared beliefs, gives form to the activities and ideas of a society. More specifically, "an order will be called *law*, if it is externally guaranteed by the probability that coercion (physical or psychological), to bring about conformity or avenge isolation, will be applied by a *staff* of people holding themselves specifically ready for that purpose" (Weber 1954, p. 5). As is true of all aspects of Weber's work, he begins with an elaborate set of definitions concerning the meaning of the *sociological* study of law, which in essence represents a specification, or an elaboration, of the legitimate order.

18. This tradition, in Weber's terms, represents an "irrational-substantive/ material law" (Freund 1968; Reinstein 1954). Law is irrational insofar as it is not based upon logic or evidence, but rather based upon what Weber refers to in other contexts as traditional: "Since the particular question at issue has always been settled in the manner ordered by God, it is necessary to settle it in a similar way" (Weber 1954, p. 260). Therefore, according to Weber, such processes cannot be controlled by the intellect. On the other hand, law is rational insofar as it is guided by general rules that are capable of control and interpretation through reasoning, calculation, and thought. Law is substantive insofar as

it tends to be empirical, taking account of circumstances not necessarily or purely within the domain of the "rules" of law. By contrast, law may be formal: "In both substantive and procedural matters, only unambiguous general character-istics of the facts of the case are taken into account" (Weber 1954, p. 63). Taken together, irrational-substantive/material law is based upon a decision of purely "emotional" value, without reference to formal rules of law. The interpreter (judge) is guided by reactions to the individual case, and these reactions in turn define the organizing principle of this tradition. The individual case is inter-preted by a judge or jury, the jury being, as Weber points out, perhaps the most "irrational" element of this organization.

19. This theme of the centrality of the market in the affairs of the world becomes more explicit in Weber's work on law which itself reflects a develop-ment of this thought different from that in *The Protestant Ethic and the Spirit of Capitalism* (1958); in the latter Weber directly challenges Marx by arguing that reinterpretation of Calvinist principles into social beliefs was the necessary *precursor* of the rise of capitalism.

20. To emphasize this point, Gerth and Mills write, "the more Weber comes to an analysis of the contemporary era, the more ready is he to speak of capital-ism as a unit. The unit is seen as a configuration of institutions, which by the logic of their own requirements increasingly narrow the range of effective choices open to men" (1946, p. 65).

4

The Voice of Tradition: The Right to Legal Representation

Lawyers comprise a key group in the administration of justice in American society (Jacob 1965). What about the benefits, in terms of income and work, that lawyers receive from their labor in the court? It has been argued that part of the court's formation rests upon "rings or cliques" that control bankruptcy procedures: "These rings embrace the referees in bankruptcy, as well as the attorneys who practice before them, the trustees and receivers, the appraisers and auctioneers, and all the other personnel who are regular participants in bankruptcy liquidations and reorganization" (Kennedy 1975, p. 399).

The Court's Organizational Matrix: 1950 to 1970

The development of these cliques or rings is explained in part by social, economic, and political developments in the court's environment, and in particular by the dimensions of industrial development. "As capitalism becomes more complex . . . entire industries come into existence whose activity is concerned with nothing but the transfer of values and the accounting entitled by this" (Braverman 1974, p. 303; also see Edwards 1972, 1975; Marglin 1974). The development of industries to take account of profit, or the failure to generate profit, finds its role in the context of the bankruptcy court.

Whereas the "old middle class" was outside the bipolar class structure and played no direct role in the accumulation of capital, the "new middle class" owes its very existence to the fact that it is central to the processes of capital accumulation (Braverman 1974; Nicolaus 1967, 1973; O'Connor 1975). The work of this new middle class depends upon the needs of the capitalist structure to strictly account for profit and loss. The role of the organizational matrix of the bankruptcy court is, in fact, to take account of this very process: the *trustees* control the bankrupts' assets while their cases are before the court; some lawyers represent *creditors* who face a loss if bankruptcy results; some lawyers represent *bankrupts* when their creditors file suit or the bankrupt parties themselves file papers to initiate bankruptcy.

While Braverman (1974) and others have referred to this middle layer of the larger class structure as one that benefits from profit, there are also fractions of this middle layer that may benefit from economic loss. The development of this matrix in the post–World War II period has played a crucial role in shaping the direction of this court. That is, those segments of the legal profession that benefit from and are tied to the present structure of the court may provide critical information for the debates on reform. To what extent are these ties to the administration of justice based upon purely impartial considerations of their role in the legal division of labor, and to what extent are they based upon strongly held vested interests? The role of lawyers and trustees—the organizational matrix—in both the development and reform of this court addresses this issue.

Central to Weber's analysis of the internal processes of modern organizations is the increasingly hierarchical division of labor for coordinating tasks. But it is also necessary to analyze organizations in their ecological-demographic setting rather than as circumscribed and closed units. The U.S. Federal District is the unit of analysis. Hence it becomes apparent that a division of labor develops not only within the organization itself but also external to the bankruptcy court. By relying upon the court's environmental profile as the unit of analysis it is possible to incorporate personnel structures that are not employed by the organization but that have, nevertheless, directly affected the development of the court. Parenthetically, one might argue that the court can be distinguished from many other types of modern organizations because of its relatively simplified division of labor; however, the incorporation of the concept of an organizational matrix suggests that this division may occur outside the formal boundaries of the organization and nevertheless have an impact upon how tasks are processed.

In sum, the organizational matrix accounts for the earnings of lawyers who represent both the bankrupt and creditor parties as well as the earnings of the trustees who are hired by the court to handle and to distribute the assets during bankruptcy proceedings.

Table 4–1 shows the total earnings of the organizational matrix of the court, the separate and relative earnings of lawyers for creditors and debtors, and of trustees, as well as the average cost of a bankruptcy proceeding. The average income of the organizational matrix measures the relative cost of a bankruptcy case for the court's clients—the bankrupt party. The average specifies, therefore, the relative cost of initiating and filing bankruptcy. While the court charges an initiation fee to file bankruptcy papers (see *U.S. Code, Title 11, Section 68* 1971), the average cost reveals the degree to which lawyers' fees, etc. (not included in the fixed court cost) are explained by social and economic factors of the community surrounding the court. The total earnings as well as the separate earnings of trustees and lawyers for creditors and debtors have increased dramatically in the decades since 1950. Moreover, the largest increase for the total, and for each group, occurred from 1950 to 1960; while there was an increase in each category from 1960 to 1970, it was less significant. By contrast, the average legal cost of a bankruptcy proceeding has remained relatively stable, with a slight decrease from 1950 to 1960.

Table 4-1
The Court's Organizational Matrix:
Lawyers and Trustees[a]

	Total		Average	
1950	1,245		37.28	
1960	3,257		29.60	
1970	5,760		29.63	
	Lawyers for creditors	*%*	*Lawyers for bankrupts*	*%*
1950	171	14	424	34
1960	307	09	1,000	31
1970	460	08	1,300	23
	Trustees	*%*		
1950	650	52		
1960	1,950	60		
1970	4,000	69		

[a]Shown in thousands.

The organizational matrix is not directly employed by this court; rather, bankruptcy cases may be one among many sources of income for these lawyers and trustees.[1] How important then are these cases for the legal community?

Lawyers, like doctors, often specialize in a specific area, though the ideology of the professional is that all are part of one occupation. Specialization within the professions, particularly medicine and law, is often another word, then, for the reification of a stratified hierarchy (Freidson 1972). This contradiction is particularly apparent in law since it is the lawyer's role to preserve the right of equal justice under the law for all citizens. Moreover, the various strata within this hierarchy have structurally different degrees of access to income, that is, to more lucrative cases.

The transformation of capitalism gave part of the legal profession a historically new and central role to play in the political economy. Symbolized by the business contract (Weber 1954) and the formation of the firm, the lawyer's role became that of a day-to-day participant in business negotiations. That is, the lawyer became more than a provider of advice and counsel in moments of crisis: "The successful modern lawyer no longer was the last resort of a businessman facing destruction, but his constant consultant at every stage of business enterprise" (Auerbach 1976, p. 36).

The lawyer as consultant contradicts the tradition of Anglo-American law.

American courts are passive: the court, as an organization, responds to, rather than initiates, social processes (Black 1973, 1976; Hurst 1965; Heydebrand, 1977b; Heydebrand and Seron, forthcoming). But modern firms often have little contact with courts; in fact, litigation departments of more prestigious firms are commonly viewed as an incidental service to clients (Smigel 1964).

Most bankruptcy cases and the court that hears such cases are part of the passive, responsive tradition of American civil law. Hence, most lawyers in this field specialize in an area that is peripheral to the "top" of their profession; they are not members of large firms that handle major corporate questions. Of course the notable exception to this is the area of corporate reorganization—the legal procedure that is perhaps feasible one step before "destruction" for those lawyers who are, in most situations, business consultants.

Insofar as lawyers of the Wall Street firm dominate the profession, their position sets the tacit standard of aspiration for the vast majority of this occupation. And the bankruptcy bar—the organizational matrix of this court—is specialized but structurally without access to major influence given the strata of people who go bankrupt, and its relationship of this area to the larger field of civil and corporate law; this relationship is symbolized by a traditional dependence upon the court for the resolution of a case.

Yet what factors explain the development of a specialized bankruptcy bar and to what extent is specialization then used as a political tactic to maintain control of the existent structure and to give these lawyers an opportunity to improve their status within the profession?

The Political Economy and the Organizational Matrix: 1950 to 1970

Table 4-2 shows zero-order correlations between measures of the monopoly sector, competitive sector, white-collar structure, and demographic patterns, and the total and average earnings per case of the organizational matrix in 1950, 1960, and 1970. In this table, the organizational matrix is measured along two dimensions. The first indicator measures the total amount earned by lawyers for the bankrupt, by lawyers for the creditor, and by trustees per district. The second indicator measures the average amount of income earned by such persons per case.

From 1950 to 1970, the zero-order correlations between most measures of the court's environment and total earnings increase. The monopoly sector is not directly subject to bankruptcy; however, merger does account for the business cases of the court (see chapter 3). Moreover, the moderately strong zero-order correlations between the total earnings of this matrix of professionals in 1960 ($r = .63$) and 1970 ($r = .69$) and merger suggest that economic complexity is an important precondition for the development of a sophisticated and specialized bankruptcy bar within a district.

Table 4-2
Zero-Order Correlations (Pearson's *r*) between Organizational Matrix
and Bankruptcy Court Environment in 1950, 1960, and 1970

	Total earnings			Average		
	'50	'60	'70	'50	'60	'70
Monopoly sector						
Merger (#)	–	.63	.69	–	.03	.51
Assets ($)	–	.03	–.05	–	.18	–.09
Competitive sector						
Manufacturing	.38	.61	.57	.06	.03	.35
Mining	–	.09	.33	–	.09	–.09
Agriculture	–	–	.23	.12	–	.06
White collar						
# White collar	–	.35	.35	–	.05	.10
# Govt. employees	–	.67	.69	–	.08	.09
Median education	.11	.28	.32	–.13	–.20	.03
Median income	.25	.07	.39	–.10	–.18	.13
Savings capital	–	.39	.80	–	.06	.13
Demographic patterns						
Population size	.23	.25	.67	.01	.05	.08
Population density	.42	.34	.38	–.13	.07	.36
Net migration	–	.52	.61	–	.04	.04

Mass immigration, industrialization, and urbanization were all manifestations of American capitalist development; with that transformation, "Lincoln's country lawyer receded into national memory" and became a symbol of a bygone era (Auerbach 1976, p. 16). Like the old middle class itself, lawyers who did not, in some way, contribute to the circulation of capital lost their economic advantage. Therefore, specialized lawyers, for example bankruptcy lawyers, are part of the newer middle class—that class which owes its existence to the surplus accumulation of capital, i.e., to the monopolization of capital (Nicolaus 1973). Thus, the "rings and cliques" of bankruptcy lawyers and trustees who work in this court are not part of a more pastoral, "simpler" legal field. Rather they are urban (1970 population size, *r* = .67; net migration, *r* = .61) lawyers who have carved out a niche in a highly stratified profession; that is, they are one professional response to the dominant interests of monopoly capital.

The competitive sector, as measured by manufacturing, is also associated with total earnings of the organizational matrix. The bankruptcy court is in many respects a competitive-sector "institution;" the moderate to strong associations between manufacturing and total earnings in 1950 (*r* = .38), 1960 (*r* = .61), and 1970 (*r* = .57) support this point.

Government employees are moderately to strongly associated with the total earnings of bankruptcy professionals in 1960 ($r = .67$) and 1970 ($r = .69$). Since the public-sector work force is a primary factor in an explanation of most task demands on the court (see chapter 3), its relatively comparable effect on the organizational matrix is not surprising. However, by 1970 the savings capital of a district also emerges as a crucial factor ($r = .80$). Bankruptcy is, it will be recalled, a lower-middle-class legal procedure. The often scant assets, however, of these workers appear to be an important precondition for the formation of a cohesive bankruptcy bar.

Until 1970 the average cost of bankruptcy to the client was not associated with measures of the court's environment. However, by 1970 the low to moderate associations between merger ($r = .51$), manufacturing ($r = .35$), and population density ($r = .36$) suggest that client costs for bankruptcy were becoming increasingly controlled by structural factors of the larger district. While bankruptcy per se is hardly a new legal procedure, the organization of this court is, in many respects, a relatively recent arrival to the judicial area. Considered in this light, it is not surprising that the average cost of a case was standardized at a rather recent point in time. After all, the organizational matrix is an informal group of lawyers and trustees, thus needing time and contact to establish itself as a clearly defined and integrated group with a clear-cut stake in the activities of this court. The cohesiveness of the bankruptcy bar is also a political question, for it remains to be seen exactly how important it is in an explanation of the size and resources of the court. We will return to this point in chapter 5.

What of the relative effect of economic and social variables in an explanation of the organizational matrix? Table 4-3 shows the separate (b^*) and joint (R^2) effect of selected environmental measures on the total earnings of the organizational matrix and the average cost to the bankrupt client in 1950, 1960, and 1970.

Total Organizational Matrix

By 1960 the environmental variables of the bankruptcy court explain over one-half of the variance in the total earnings of the organizational matrix ($R^2 = .61$) and suggest that the professionals of the bankruptcy court have long been a critical factor in understanding this organization. (Note, however, that data for the number of mergers and government employees are not available in 1950; however, the environmental measures for 1960 and 1970 are exactly comparable.)

Moreover, the standardized regression coefficients essentially confirm the analysis of zero-order correlations discussed above. That is, the direct effect of merger in 1960 ($b^* = .43$) and 1970 ($b^* = .44$) along with government employees, again in 1960 ($b^* = .52$) and 1970 ($b^* = .48$), is moderate. In essence, the

Table 4-3

Zero-Order Correlations (r), Standardized Regression Coefficients   and Squared Multiple Correlation Coefficients (R^2) of Five Environmental Variables on the Organizational Matrix of the Bankruptcy Court in 1950, 1960, and 1970

		Total organizational matrix			Average of organizational matrix		
		'50	'60	'70	'50	'60	'70
Merger	r	—	.63	.69	—	.03	.51
	$b*$	—	.43	.44	—	.06	.52
Manufacturing	r	.38	.61	.57	.06	.03	.35
	$b*$	.25	.13	.23	.15	—.11	.01
Govt. employees	r	—	.67	.69	—	.08	.09
	$b*$	—	.52	.48	—	.21	—.13
Median education	r	.11	.28	.32	—.13	—.20	.03
	$b*$	.06	.01	.10	—.11	—.24	—.12
Population density	r	.42	.34	.38	—.13	.07	.36
	$b*$	.30	—.29	—.20	—.18	—	.13
	R^2	.22	.61	.72	.05	.06	.30

formation of a cohesive bankruptcy bar is a response to the dominant nexus of the late twentieth century, i.e., the mutual dependence of the private and public sectors. Whereas the caseload and casemix is, in part, still explained by the traditional and older competitive-sector measures (see tables 3-3 and 3-4), the formation of a professional middle class—for example, the organizational matrix of the bankruptcy court—occurs because it continues to serve the needs of contemporary capitalist development: the circulation and accumulation of capital.

Finally, these findings do emphasize and make clear the fact that the organizational matrix was, and has been for a significant period of time, dependent upon the present formation of the court. Moreover, its dependence upon this arrangement may have significant implications in the process of court reform since organizational change may redefine the professional's relationship to this court. The implication of this dependence, however, is a political question that must also be understood as a negotiated process of reform.

The Average Cost

The emerging pattern between the respective measures of the organizational matrix and the court's environment suggests that the source of total income to these personnel was circumscribed at an earlier point in time than the average cost to the client.

In 1950 (R^2 = .05) and 1960 (R^2 = .06), the measures of the court's environment did not explain the cost to the bankrupt party. By 1970, these measures explain over one-fourth (R^2 = .30) of the variance in this measure. Again, the standardized regression coefficients confirm the zero-order correlations and suggest that monopoly-sector activity, i.e., merger (b^* = .52), is the primary factor in an explanation of the average cost of bankruptcy proceedings. The organizational matrix may no longer be an unintegrated group of lawyers and trustees; in fact, the findings indicate that quite the contrary may be the case. With twenty years of work for the legal profession, the interests of this group may be much more clearly defined.

Reform of the bankruptcy court involves the possibility of restructuring the organizational process of this legal procedure; moreover, the reorganization of the court may eliminate the need for lawyers as representatives of clients and trustees as representatives of creditors in most cases. The introduction of an administrative organization to process bankruptcy cases challenges the adversary process of the court and hence its need for lawyers. If it can be shown that a bankruptcy case does not require legal representation, then it may be possible to show that legal representation is not necessary in other types of disputes as well. Herein lies the fundamental challenge that the legal profession, the organizational matrix of the bankruptcy court, must confront in the process of court reform. But, in the process of reform, the legal profession is directly represented whereas the client in indirectly represented. That is, the representatives of the bankruptcy bar enter the political arena to debate the reform of the court at a clear and dramatic advantage over the representatives of bankrupt clients.

The Organizational Matrix: Local versus Cosmopolitan

The organizational matrix has played a central role in the development of the court. The Commission's Bill seeks to minimize the role of lawyers and trustees whereas the Judges' Bill seeks to maintain or enhance their role.

Debates around these alternative roles for lawyers and trustees in the future of the bankruptcy court may fundamentally challenge the present collegial relations of the court. Are the clients of the court better served by a centralized administrative agency that potentially minimizes the need for most lawyers and trustees or by a decentralized collegial organization that emphasizes the role of lawyers and trustees?

The bankruptcy bar and its other specialists perform a service; hence, they depend upon this court for the organization of their livelihood. It is quite difficult to organize private legal services into large-scale units analogous to those developed around productive labor (O'Connor 1975). Hence, service organizations and professions tend to reflect the local mores of an area; for example, courts—a public service organization—have commonly mirrored the race relations of a region such that southern federal courts have, at earlier points in history, been formally segregated (Richardson and Vines 1970).

However, there seems to be some "tension between a [service] organization's bureaucratic needs for expertise and its social-system needs for loyalty" (Gouldner 1958, p. 446).[2] The dialogue between "locals" and "cosmopolitans" may be one way for an organization to meet these potentially conflicting demands. That is, locals fulfill an organization's need for "loyal" members whereas cosmopolitans fulfill an organization's need for "expert" members. Cosmopolitans—the experts—are more committed to a job than they are to an organization. Locals—the loyals—are more committed to an organization than they are to a job.

However, local-cosmopolitan orientations derive from a group's political, social, and economic position in an organization. In the case of the bankruptcy court, lawyers, judges, and creditors represent a local orientation. They are committed to the organization of the bankruptcy court because, as has been shown throughout this book, they benefit from that organization. And, in Gouldner's terms, they are loyal organizational members. Consumer law advocates, legal scholars, and organized labor represent a cosmopolitan orientation. They are respectively committed to consumers, law, and workers. And, in Gouldner's terms, they are expert organizational members. Therefore, local-cosmopolitan positions may also have important political-organizational implications. A decentralized collegial court structure (that relies upon lawyers, judges, and trustees) complements the demands of most locals (lawyers, judges, and creditors). A centralized administrative agency (that minimizes the role of judges, lawyers, and trustees) complements the demands of most cosmopolitans (consumer law advocates, legal scholars, and organized labor). Therefore, the dialogue between locals and cosmopolitans provides a point of departure for analyzing the ways in which various interest groups involved in court reform interpret the place of lawyers and trustees—the organizational matrix—in the future of the bankruptcy court.[3]

The locals are represented by those professionals who perform crucial services for this court; the organizing link of their labor is the role they perform vis-à-vis this court. Hence, these professionals, like other types of service professionals, particularly doctors, find a centralized hierarchical organization antithetical to their political interests and needs.

The Locals

The locals, represented by judges, creditors, and lawyers, state that the bankruptcy process should continue to incorporate lawyers and trustees in the processing of all bankruptcy cases. Judges, creditors, and lawyers come to the debates on court reform as participants in the day-to-day activities of the bankruptcy court. In large part, their right to enter the debates on reform rests upon personal contact with the bankruptcy court that has resulted in a strong local network circumscribed by the district of the court. Thus, they come to the national debate as representatives from local areas.

Judges: As stated by the judges, the maintenance of lawyers and trustees indirectly supports their overall position insofar as they seek to upgrade the prestige of the bankruptcy court. To support this position, the judges argue that under the system proposed by the Judges' Bill, the local court of an area would maintain a list of lawyers qualified to guide a bankrupt client in the filing of appropriate forms. This list would be compiled in consultation with the bar association of an area.

Removal of adequate support from trustees and lawyers, as suggested by the Commission's Bill, would destroy the capacity of bankruptcy proceedings to meet the needs of individual cases. Or, as one judge argued, "The greatest cost attendant upon the adoption of the Commission recommendation would be the creation of an insolvency process stripped of its social and economic relevance and of its capacity to improvise and implement appropriate remedies in the light and context of individual circumstances" (*Senate Hearings* 1975, p. 103; [emphasis not added;], also see *House Hearings* 1975, pp. 210–23). According to judges, bankruptcy procedure must continue to provide a forum that adequately meets the demands generated by each and every case. Without the support services of trustees and lawyers, this is not possible; thus, "the selection of a trustee under the Commission's Bill seems unnecessarily difficult and cumbersome" (*House Hearings* 1976, p. 1574).

Creditors: Creditors, of course, are directly affected by the proposals suggested by the Commission. Their argument in support of the Judges' Bill rests upon the assumption that making the consumer bankruptcy process an administrative procedure would result in a "bankruptcy explosion:"[4] "By making consumer bankruptcy strictly an administrative process many consumers may be encouraged to petition bankruptcy when they really don't need that relief" (*Senate Hearings* 1975, p. 193; also see *House Hearings* 1976, pp. 897–908). Creditors imply that presently a lawyer's fee discourages needless bankruptcy filings. Without that protective device there would be unnecessary and unjustifiable reliance upon bankruptcy.

Most creditors' representatives go on to argue that the Commission's Bill favors the bankrupt and gives little support to the legal rights of creditors: creditors should continue to have the "same free and unrestricted right which they now have to select a trustee in any kind of case and to elect a creditor's committee in rehabilitation chapter cases" (*Senate Hearings* 1975, p. 428). By denying this right to creditors, the bankruptcy process explicitly favors the consumer over the creditor. It is questionable, they suggest, whether such a policy is constitutional.

Representatives of banking make a similar point with regard to business lending, claiming that "Unless the proposals are amended to insure creditors protection no less than that presently enjoyed, the nature of commercial bank lending—indeed of all secured lending—will be permanently altered" (*House Hearings* 1976, p. 2500; also see *House Hearings* 1976, p. 1667; *Senate Hearings* 1975, pp. 427-53). On this point creditors concerned with consumer and business bankruptcies take a basically similar position.

Finally, the argument of creditors continues the credit industry in the post-World War II period has supported an important social "service" to the poor by providing ready access to money. If the Commission's Bill is enacted, credit companies will be forced to curtail loans to this low-income bracket, thus cutting off a vitally needed service. (Also see *House Hearings* 1976, pp. 1666-74.)

Practicing Attorneys: Like creditors, attorneys who have worked in the area of bankruptcy law support the Judges' Bill. These lawyers suggest that clerks in an agency, as proposed by the Commission's Bill, cannot fill out forms any less expensively than clerks working in a private law firm. Therefore, the assumption that the Commission's Bill would save money is unfounded:

The Commission Report attempts to justify the cost of the new bureaucracy by eliminating the expense to the debtor of hiring an attorney. Aside from the questionable desirability of shifting the cost from the individuals who use the system to the general public by taxation, we are not convinced that there would be cost reduction in any event. (*Senate Hearings* 1975, p. 580; also see *House Hearings* 1976, pp. 1263, 1398–1402, 1424–40)

Lawyers who have worked in this area are trained to process bankruptcy cases; they argue that at a time when the dockets of bankruptcy courts are increasing at a marked pace, society cannot afford to develop a new system inundated with cases when there is no time to solve such an agency's problems.

A centralized agency, as proposed by the Commission, will sacrifice the ability to respond to local needs and attitudes. Thus, one lawyer states,

Any centralized administrative authority will have the disadvantages of lack of responsiveness, inefficiency, expense, geographical remoteness, lack of understanding of local needs and of local business and judicial environment, as well as all of the evils of a far-removed bureaucracy without any of the advantages that centralized government can provide. (*Senate Hearings* 1975, p. 555)

This is a large country, the lawyers argue, with many distinct and peculiar characteristics. Therefore, the bankruptcy process must be organizationally adaptive. This is possible only through a court house structure as proposed by the judges.

The place for specialization, these attorneys argue, is in the lawyer's office: "Specialization, of course, not only develops expertise in the attorney but allows him to develop a staff with expertise. He is able to use paralegals, but as in a doctor's office, it should be remembered that it is not the nurse you go to for medical counseling, but the doctor" (*House Hearings* 1976, p. 1264). Thus, specialization in itself is not opposed, so long as it is controlled by the legal profession (also see *House Hearings* 1976, p. 1257).

Lawyers also state that those who have worked in the area know that the initiation of bankruptcy procedure is often a traumatic and frightening experience for the client. At this moment, the client needs the individual service and advice obtainable only from a lawyer trained in the area. Without this support from lawyers, the law "will serve to further remove 'little people,' whether debtors or creditors, from the courts. We decry that concept since we believe that the courts have traditionally been the best guardian of the rights and liberties of the people of the United States" (*Senate Hearings* 1975, p. 533; also see *House Hearings* 1975, pp. 1651–66). The court has been the protector of individual rights in American society (*House Hearings* 1976, p. 1263). These rights are protected regardless of what the case may be. Thus, lawyers conclude by arguing that without a *local* bankruptcy court to protect these rights, the government is instituting an explicit system of preference. That is, the court ceases to provide a forum for all of its citizenry. (But also see *Senate Hearings* 1975, pp. 389–425.)

Judges, creditors, and lawyers support a local, decentralized court system for the processing of bankruptcy cases. They claim that the reform of bankruptcy practices must continue to respond to the unique characteristics of specific areas. Denying the bankrupt client access to private legal counsel and denying creditors the right to elect their own trustee (*House Hearings* 1976, p. 1539; *Senate Hearings* 1975, pp. 533–52) destroys the court's ability to be responsive to each individual case.[5] By implication, these interest groups suggest that the needs of potential bankrupts are unique from region to region. They conclude that this law must protect and guarantee the rights of all individuals to go bankrupt and, perhaps more importantly, all creditors to recover their debts.

The Cosmopolitans

The cosmopolitan is represented by consumer law advocates, representatives of labor, and legal scholars. These groups were outsiders in the development of the court: they have not been day-to-day participants in bankruptcy cases. Legitimation of their right to speak to the issues concerning bankruptcy reform is based upon other credentials. In the case of labor, it is based upon a historical struggle resulting in a strong bargaining position with employers (see McConnel 1966). In the case of consumer law advocates, it is based upon successful legal work in other areas of consumer concerns. And, in the case of legal scholars, it is based upon a prestigious career within the academy.

Legal Scholars: The cosmopolitan position, as stated by legal scholars, revolves around two issues: the sporadic reliance upon Chapter XIII procedures, as against straight bankruptcy, and the role of lawyers in the bankruptcy process.

Earlier findings showed that Chapter XIII cases (consumer reorganization), unlike any other aspect of the court's work, did not differ from district to district in correlation with economic and population characteristics. It was inferred from these findings that the initiation of such procedures may have more to do with the attitude of judges and the local bar of a district than with the economy surrounding the court. The testimony of one legal scholar confirms this assumption (*House Hearings* 1975, p. 168; also see *House Hearings* 1976, pp. 766-88). The Commission thought it objectionable that such cases rested upon such individual criteria. However, consumer reorganization procedure must remain one legal option among others. Therefore, it proposes to standardize the use of this procedure; legal counseling should be an activity internal to the administration of bankruptcy itself. The only way that this procedure can be used in a justifiable way is through a formalized and centralized process of counseling that insures against its presently sporadic use.

A representative of legal scholars also suggests that "bankruptcy has one dominant purpose for debtors and another for creditors" (*House Hearings* 1975, p. 157; also see *House Hearings* 1975, pp. 330-44, 766-88). The history of legal decision making and Congressional amendments has sought to equalize the interests of these two parties. Seen in this light, the Commission's Bill is another step in the equalizing process. As the organization of bankruptcy presently exists, debtors are at a disadvantage both inside and outside the court. They are at a disadvantage outside the court insofar as the credit industry selects its location strategically. As one legal scholar put the case, "The choice of market location, the size and terms of the typical location, the nature and placements of advertising, and other such factors will reveal what I believe is a consistent stratification in the consumer credit business; not quite women's ready to wear, but discernible" (Shuchman 1973–1974, p. 428; also reprinted in *House Hearings* 1975). Once the debtors enter the court to settle disputes with creditors, they remain at a disadvantage due to the unsystematic way in which information for a case is presently collected:[6]

The process of checking on assets was very unsystematic, using the private appraisers or trustees. Often they would look at the address and decide that they were not going to bother because nobody in the neighborhood had anything; in other cases they might be new law school graduates, who were very diligent in going out and checking under every pebble. But, in any event, it is very uneven in the private system, and we think it would be better to have somebody who is skilled at assessing evaluation and who would do that as a full-time job. (*House Hearings* 1975, pp. 381–82)

The Commission's Bill seeks to correct these problems by minimizing reliance upon attorneys or trustees from the private sector. Thus, the legal scholars go on to argue that "the real basis for the opposition [from lawyers] will be loss of income which they [lawyers] foresee. . . . Attorneys may have to be more openminded about the ways in which they work. There will still be roles for attorneys in this sytem" (*House Hearings* 1975, pp. 386–87).

Legal scholars suggest that the overall picture reveals that the debtor is at a disadvantage in the present system and that the bar has not taken a responsible role in this area of the law. Therefore, the solution is twofold: to eliminate both trustees and lawyers, and to control both the counseling and processing that bankruptcy cases demand through a centralized organizational structure.

Consumer Law Groups: Consumer law advocates state their support for the elimination of the role of trustees in straightforward terms: "It does seem to us that the cost of case management is increased when trustees are statutorily required. Since that cost is passed on to the debtor where possible, we are concerned that something that is unnecessary or inappropriate may be required by statute" (*Senate Hearings* 1975, p. 309). Consumer law advocates also take the position that civil-servant counseling of consumers, as opposed to legal counseling by attorneys, is a degradation of the consumer (*House Hearings* 1976, pp. 1337–41). But this is not to suggest that these advocates of consumers' rights are totally unaware of shady legal practices by members of their profession. In response to this, one advocate states that "I have observed that some bankruptcy practitioners charge reasonable attorney's fees for the bankruptcy itself, and then 'nickel and dime' the client by post-filing charges which in fact are never reported to bankruptcy judges" (*House Hearings* 1976, p. 1340). Thus, reform should include more exacting procedures for reporting attorney's fees. This proposal, like others presented by consumer advocates, is, however, often made by a lone voice with little support from other interest groups. Thus, as a group they do not fully support the Commission's Bill.[7] But their position with regard to trustees is clear: they are an expense to the consumer that is unnecessary and should be eliminated.

Organized Labor: Labor representatives are concerned primarily with the protection of workers in the case of corporate bankruptcy. As the system presently exists, the workers in such firms are not adequately protected if a company goes bankrupt. From their point of view, the law structurally protects creditors without concern for workers: "The supplier of goods and products to the employer may protect himself if he believes his customer's financial position is perilous. He may limit credit, require cash on the barrelhead, or arrange for a security interest with his corporate customer. The worker has no such options" (*Senate Hearings* 1975, p. 294). As was shown earlier, the redefinition of laws (i.e., wage laws) is the only vehicle that labor suggests as a viable tool for correcting these inequities. (Also see *House Hearings* 1976, pp. 2421-53.)

The cosmopolitan position is most broadly stated by legal scholars. Both consumer law advocates and representatives of labor take a more narrow perspective by primarily criticizing the present structure. However, support for a more centralized organization that can minimize trustees and lawyers is supported by the representatives of labor and consumer law advocates on the grounds that consumer bankrupts are at a disadvantage under the present system.

Conclusion: The Future of the Organizational Matrix

In many respects, political debate over the role of the organizational matrix parallels the earlier analysis of task demand. That is, those groups that have played a part in the court's development argue that the demands on the court are the result of an open-credit economy. They conclude that reform must provide mechanisms to protect credtiors if this industry is to provide an on-going social service to lower-income groups. By contrast, most interest groups that have been outside the development of the court conclude that lawyers and trustees must be eliminated from the organization of bankruptcy in the name of court reform. Thus, there is a rather consistent pattern to the debate on organizational change. Various interest groups seek to take the reform of the court into their own hands for their own ends.

In large part, lawyers support the judges because of their affiliation and dependence upon the present structure of the court. Considering a more historical perspective, Weber suggests that

the vocational responsibility of maintaining the existing legal system seems to place the practitioners of the law in general among the "conservative" forces. This is true in the twofold sense that legal practitioners are inclined to remain cool not only toward the pressures of substantive postulates put forward from "below" in the name of "social" ideals but also toward those from "above" which are put forward in the name of patriarchal power, or the welfare interests of the sovereign. (Weber 1954, p. 298)

In general, Weber suggests that lawyers tend to support the maintenance of the status quo. In the case before us, this certainly seems to be true. The history of bankruptcy places creditors in a position comparable to that of lawyers; hence their similar political stance.

The legal profession has historically opposed the introduction of administrative agencies, though they have certainly reaped the benefits of these reforms (Auerbach 1976). During the New Deal period the legal establishment viewed administrative law as a threat to the traditions of American democracy, yet this profession has successfully used such laws to legitimate the further monopolization of capital and in turn secured a pivotal role for attorneys. In spite of the legal profession's successful control over administrative law and reforms, they continue to oppose its introduction in the area of bankruptcy law. Their position is based upon the apparent threat of their immediate relationship to the court, though experience has shown that attorneys have continued to control the administration of legal disputes even when such reforms have been successfully introduced in other areas.

Notes

1. Bankruptcy is, therefore, like other U.S. federal question and diversity cases but unlike criminal and U.S. cases. That is, lawyers in bankruptcy court are from the "private" bar. However, in most courts a very specialized group of such lawyers has developed who control, by default, bankruptcy proceedings. In the process of reform the desirability of this specialized bar is a primary source of political tension among various groups.

2. Reissman (1940) studied the social roles of bureaucrats in a civil-service setting. In that study, he developed a typology of four roles of bureaucrats: the "functional bureaucrat," who is oriented toward a professional group but works in a hierarchical organizational setting; the "specialist bureaucrat," who is oriented toward a profession but with a keen identity with the organization; the "service bureaucrat," who selects to work in a bureaucratic, public setting because of the "good" work that is possible (e.g. working for handicapped children); and the "job bureaucrat," who has an orientation which is clearly identified with the work setting. In Gouldner's terms, the functional bureaucrat and the specialist bureaucrat are cosmopolitans; the service bureaucrat and the job bureaucrat are locals. However, both Reissman and Gouldner develop their respective typologies from a perspective of social roles. I am suggesting that such orientations are also associated with an individual's social, political, and economic status in an organization; the concept of locals and cosmopolitans is one way to consider the distillation of various groups' social, economic, and political orientation toward organizational change.

3. As Merton (1966) points out in his discussion of influentials, locals and cosmopolitans may be of the same profession but have different orientations toward that profession. This is clearly the case in this study. Consumer law

advocates and representatives of the organizational matrix are, in many instances, lawyers; however, their respective work settings have yielded very different positions on issues related to court reform.

4. The testimony of practicing attorneys makes the same point (*House Hearings* 1976, p. 1265).

5. The Security and Exchange Commission (SEC) also supports the maintenance of trustees, specifically in large, publicly owned corporations (*House Hearings* 1976, p. 2212). The representative from the SEC presents an interesting point because his position underscores the structural advantage of business over consumer interests in the debates on reform. (Also see *House Hearings* 1976, pp. 2214–26; *Senate Hearings* 1975, pp. 707–81.)

6. Testimony by a representative from the Federal Trade Commission (FTC) also supports this point:

In personal bankruptcies, where trustees are routinely appointed in what appear to be no-asset cases, the present system of bankruptcy law permits the trustee—encourages him—to convert those matters into nominal asset cases. . . . The trustee can ferret out enough "property" to create a fund from which in the typical case there will be enough to pay him substantially more than the $10 statutory fee. But rarely will the estate so created be large enough to pay any significant sums (or pay anything at all) to general or unsecured creditors (*House Hearings,* 1976, p. 773).

Like other representatives from agencies of the executive branch, the FTC takes a stand primarily on this issue. A representative from the U.S. Attorney's Office, supporting the Commission, takes a similar position to that elaborated by this representative from the FTC (*House Hearings* 1976, p. 2099).

7. However, this position of consumer law advocates does suggest that they tend to identify more strongly with lawyers, other members of their profession, than with consumers, their clients.

5 Bureaucratization, Professionalization, or Computerization?

The caseload, casemix, and matrix of professionals in the bankruptcy court are explained by the changing environmental profile of the several districts. The nexus of the court's task environment reflects various developments in the competitive, monopoly, and state sectors. Whereas the caseload and casemix clarify the court's relationship to the competitive sector and its responsiveness to this older, more traditional facet of the economy, the matrix of professionals who depend upon this court for a livelihood—lawyers and trustees—are, in part, explained by the growth of the monopoly sector. Finally, the rise of the state sector is a critical factor in understanding both of these elements in the bankruptcy court. It is also clear that the definition of demand and professional responsibility vis-á-vis this court are actually political questions open for negotiation in the process of reform.

While the task environment sets the stage for this organization, the court's size and resources are the hub of its structure. Courts are labor-intensive, professional service organizations (Heydebrand, 1977b). This means that its service—the adjudication and administration of bankruptcy procedure—is a more 'rational' refinement of the service of the traditional court, a development that is increasingly common in numerous parts of the judiciary (Schubert 1960).

Insofar as this court is specialized, it represents one organizational response to urbanization, industrialization, and bureaucratization of the state sector. Ironically, though, these economic, social, and demographic developments are also the source of the court's congestion, delay and the consequent call for reform. The signs of rationality in the judicial branch are profound: juries are less and less common (Blumberg 1970; Heydebrand and Seron, forthcoming; Schubert 1960); experts are increasingly brought in to explain the particulars of esoteric and technical questions (Schubert 1960); specialized judges, as is the case with bankruptcy, preside over ever more narrow and specific classes of cases (Parness 1973). Thus, the separation and specialization of the bankruptcy court from the federal district court since 1938 itself represents a more common response to the double bind of the judiciary.

A number of questions must now be addressed: what has happened to the size and resources of the court? What factors of the court's task environment—its demand or its professional matrix—account for the size and resources of the court? And, finally, what issues do the size and resources of the court raise in the process of reform?

The Personnel and Resources of the Bankruptcy Court:
1950 to 1970

The judicial branch faces a dramatic problem: as the demand for its services has increased, the relative share of its budget has remained almost constant (O'Connor 1973). That is, the court system reflects, in microcism, the double bind of the state itself (Kolko 1967; O'Connor 1973; Pivan and Cloward 1971; Weinstein 1968; Williams 1961). The increasing demand for bankruptcy services coupled with the formation of a middle class of bankruptcy professionals has been documented and shown to be generated by the economic and social structure of the court's environment.

Yet the court system has received a small share of the total federal budget each decade since 1910 (Burger 1971; Heydebrand and Seron, forthcoming). For example, the judiciary received .06 percent of the total U.S. budget in 1950, 1960, and 1970, whereas the Justice Department, one part of the executive branch, received .3 percent each decade (*U.S. Budget in Brief* 1952, 1962, 1972).

It was shown in chapter 4 that courts have historically been passive organizations. This means that courts respond to demands generated by their environment; seldom do they initiate activities on their own. Yet the cases heard represent, in microcism, the social conflicts that permeate American society, from labor management questions to civil rights cases to bankruptcies. Like the newer, more modern and "rational" agencies of the executive branch (McConnell 1966) the goal of these state-sector organizations is to preserve "social harmony" (O'Connor 1973). However, the third branch, as compared to the executive branch, is a less effective social expense precisely because the courts do not have the legal authority to actively intervene in the conflicts of interest woven into the American social fabric. By contrast, executive-branch agencies may be granted this power and thus respond more "effectively" to the social, economic, and political issues of the day. In one sense the courts, then, are organizational artifacts, albeit of considerable importance (Heydebrand and Seron, forthcoming).

The bankruptcy court is a part of the judiciary: what has happened to the budget of the court in the face of these exacerbated constraints placed upon the third branch?

Table 5-1 shows the resources and judicial personnel of this court from 1950 to 1970. The resources of this court derive from two sources: *receipts* from cases that come before the court and *allocations* from Congress that are part of the larger U.S. budget. Historically, the bankruptcy court was a self-supporting organization since the revenues accrued from cases did not exceed the expenses of operating the court. However, by 1966 the court was no longer able to fulfill this obligation (*Tables of Bankruptcy Statistics* 1969, p. 2).

Table 5-1
The Court's Personnel and Resources: 1950 to 1970

	Full-time Judges	Part-time Judges	% Full time
1950	52	110	34
1960	97	92	51
1970	181	33	85

Total resources

	Receipts	Obligations	Surplus
1950	1,844,420	1,697,420	197,000
1960	5,880,301	5,010,026	870,275
1970	11,041,534	15,573,000	−4,531,466

Total administrative costs

1950	6,826,932
1960	16,129,903
1970	26,446,037

Thus, in the past decade the bankruptcy court has required additional allocations from the Congress. As table 5-1 shows, by 1970 this amounted to 4.5 million dollars.

The obligations shown in table 5-1 represent, then, the operating budget of this court whereas the receipts are the monetary holdings of the court. Two things are apparent: the budget of this court has grown dramatically but the receipts have not kept pace with the obligations of this organization. Legally, or politically, this court is an autonomous organization since it is a part of the third branch with some degree of *de jure* independence; but like the third branch itself it is not economically autonomous insofar as it lacks control over its financial resources (Heydebrand 1973b). While the court has become a more important legal forum of the third branch, it has also sacrificed a degree of legal autonomy due to its functional, or economic, dependence upon the Congress. In sum, table 5-1 shows that the court is an increasingly expensive organization to operate at a time when the state must also face numerous other pressing social expenses, e.g. welfare, defense, education, health, and so on.

However, this court has also long relied upon various nonjudicial and bureaucratic personnel in the disposition of cases. In fact, bankruptcy has historically made receivers, auctioneers, and clerks, along with lawyers, mandatory personnel in the adjudication of these cases (see *U.S. Code, Title 11, Section 102,* 1971). However, the relationship between these nonjudicial personnel varies from district to district since the judges of a court have the discretion to determine the responsibilities and fees of its support staff. The fact that these various personnel are not uniformly organized mirrors both the decentralized history and network of the larger third branch and the significant variations in demand for legal services across the several districts (Flanders 1976; Richardson and Vines 1970). Table 5-1 also shows the total costs paid to these personnel in the liquidation of asset cases in 1950, 1960, and 1970. These figures represent fees and expenses incurred in the liquidation of such cases and allowed by the court as necessary administrative expenses to be paid from the estate. It will be recalled from chapter 3 that the number of asset cases increased significantly from 1950 to 1970 (see table 3-1b); hence, it is not surprising that the cost of adjudicating and administrating such cases has also increased. However, a salient point emerges from a comparison of these two sets of figures. That is that by 1970, the administrative costs of a proportion of the total caseload—i.e., asset cases—exceeded the total obligations of this court. Yet, the increased reliance upon support staff of all kinds contradicts the collegial history of a court where the judge is unquestionably the most important figure. Are judges, however, that important?

At the core of the debate over court reform is the question of bureaucratizing bankruptcy law and procedure by establishing an administrative agency to hear such cases. It is clear, however, that the court has historically paid a high price for what may be a collegial facade since a large share of its resources have been allocated to nonjudicial personnel and support staff. Is it necessary to continue this relationship? Or are there other ways to organize the demand for bankruptcy services?

Table 5-1 shows the number of full-time and part-time bankruptcy judges as well as the persentage of full-time judges to the total judicial staff from 1950 to 1970. Though the tasks of this court are specialized, its structure complements the generalist organization of the federal district courts; that is, the judge is the anchor point of this organization.

Hence, the addition of a judge's slot remains the primary means for meeting increasingly large, variable, or complex demands. The addition of a judge's slot within a district is a political process since all such slots must be approved by the Federal Judicial Conference—the administrative arm of the federal courts. The addition of a slot, when granted, specifies either a part-time or full-time position. The decision to make the slot part-time or full-time is based upon the organizational needs and the political clout of a district. A part-time position is not, by definition, one-half of a full-time position. Such a position can vary anywhere from one-half to one-quarter time (and in some cases to less). Therefore, two part-time judges do not necessarily equal one full-time judge. In spite of these varying hiring practices, the licensing of all judges in bankruptcy is uniform insofar as formal, legal training is a prerequisite.

Thus, the judicial staff of a court confronts an interesting paradox: on the one hand there is a formal, written prerequisite for job incumbents; on the other hand, there is an informal, unwritten procedure that determines the salary of a part-time judge.

It is clear from table 5-1 that full-time judges have achieved a strong position in this court during the post-World War II period. Whereas full-time judges represented only 34 percent of the court's judicial personnel in 1950, by 1970 they represented 85 percent. In 1950, the principle figure in this court, the judge, usually worked on a part-time basis; by 1970, this was rarely the case.

The rise in the number of full-time judges also has significant implications for understanding court reform. The most important personnel of this organization now seems to form, like the matrix of professionals who depend upon this court for a livelihood, a numerically strong group. Thus, the judges of this court represent perhaps the pivotal group as reform is debated. Yet, judges stand most to lose should the Congress authorize the establishment of an administrative agency housed in the executive. Hence, their clear and consistent position, as documented in chapters 3 and 4, is not surprising. The choice of a more professional or a more bureaucratic-type organization is the core of this debate on reform: it is the heart of this conflict.

But before turning to this question it is necessary to examine the relative effect of the variables of the task environment—the caseload, case mix, and organizational matrix—in an explanation of the personnel and resources (i.e., size) of the court. Has this court grown in response to demand or in response to the formation of a cohesive matrix of professionals within the legal community?

The Task Environment, Personnel, and Resources of the Bankruptcy Court

The research conducted in organizational analysis has relied upon the variable of size primarily as a predictive variable (Anderson and Warkov 1961; Blau 1970; Heydebrand 1973a; Meyer 1972; Pondy 1969). The findings of the effects of size on organizational structure vary with such elements as the type of organization studied, the relative degree of technology, the hierarchical structure, the complexity of task, and the division of labor. The common thread in these studies is the assumption that size has a causally prior impact upon various aspects of organizational structure. However, these analyses have tended to focus upon intraorganizational relations without consideration for the causally prior aspects of the environment (but see Boland 1973). However we have already seen that in the case of an organization such as the bankruptcy court the environment is of critical importance, particularly since the court is a passive structure. That is, economic, social, and political developments in the district explain the court's task environment, i.e., the rise in bankruptcy cases and the formation of a matrix of legal professionals who depend upon the court for a living. The task environment then specifies the relationship between inter- and intraorganizational levels: whereas the organizational matrix describes the "linkage" (Pfeffer 1972a) between this court and the legal community at large, the task structure describes the actual workload of the court.

Considered in this context it becomes apparent that the size of a court (personnel and resources) is itself a response to external pressures. In fact, the addition of judges is technically the only response that the judges have available, unless the Congress uses its power to authorize the formation of a new type of organization, for instance an administrative agency, to dispose of such cases. The composition of the court's judicial staff has been transformed from part-time to full-time professionals. This represents, then, a paradigmatic shift in this organization within the parameters that the court has available.

Table 5-2 shows correlations between indicators of task and organizational matrix with the size (i.e., personnel and resources) of the bankruptcy court in 1950, 1960, and 1970.

Personnel

The number of full-time judges grew by 248 percent from 1950 to 1970. In 1950 the full-time bankruptcy judge was an exceptional figure. Table 5-2 shows that such judges were strongly associated with asset ($r = .78$) and business ($r = .73$) cases. In fact, these associations are also significantly stronger than those shown between other measures of task (i.e., caseload) and organizational matrix. However, the correlation between pending cases and full-time judges is moderate ($r = .45$); this suggests that full-time judges were more likely in more congested, or backlogged, courts; even as early as 1950, backlog was a significant organizational variable. At this relatively early point in the court's history, then, the full-time judge was primarily associated with districts described by a more complex casemix (i.e., a larger proportion of asset and business cases) and a backlogged docket.

By 1960, however, this picture had changed. First of all, full-time judges are seen to be moderately associated with the caseload of a court (pending, $r = .56$; filings, $r = .63$; demand, $r = .63$); while the respective associations with asset ($r = .61$) and business ($r = .50$) cases are less than they were in 1950, they are nevertheless still moderate. Finally, the total earnings of the court's organizational matrix is moderately to strongly associated with full-time judges ($r = .69$). In essence, it appears that the size of the caseload itself was beginning to have a more profound impact upon the court's composition of full-time judges.

In 1970, the associations between each measure of the task and organizational matrix with full-time judges was significantly stronger than that shown for

Table 5-2
Zero-Order Correlations (Pearson's r) between the Personnel and Resources and the Task Structure and Organizational Matrix of the Bankruptcy Court in 1950, 1960, and 1970

	Personnel						Resources		
	Full-time Judges			Part-time Judges			Clerks[a]	Judicial[a]	Nonjudicial[a]
	'50	'60	'70	'50	'60	'70	'70	'70	'70
Task:									
Caseload									
Pending	.45	.56	.82	.16	.07	−.10	.90	.83	.88
Filings	−.05	.63	.87	.11	−.01	−.16	.96	.88	.95
Demand	−.01	.63	.86	.13	−.04	−.13	.94	.87	.93
Casemix									
Asset	.78	.61	.75	.24	−.11	−.09	.75	.76	.71
Business	.73	.50	.75	.12	−.04	−.19	.71	.75	.69
Consumer	.25	.08	.49	.07	−.06	.02	.58	.51	.57
Organizational matrix									
Total	.56	.69	.87	.13	−.09	−.18	.85	.87	.82
Average	−.06	−.15	.11	.10	.03	.05	−.02	.11	−.04

[a] Available for 1970 only.

1960. (Note that in each decade the correlations between the average of the organizational matrix and full-time judges are insignificant.) Whereas in 1950 full-time judges were basically associated with districts that had a more complex casemix, by 1970 full-time judges were associated with all aspects of the court's task environment.

This shift from 1950 to 1970 is particularly significant in light of the correlations shown for part-time judges. In no case, at no point in time, are part-time judges associated with indicators of the court's task environment. This is rather surprising since the court was primarily composed of part-time judges in 1950; in fact, as late as 1960, only 51 percent of its judicial staff was full-time (see table 5-1). However, the consistently low correlations also suggest the reasons behind the court's shift from part-time to full-time judges. First of all, part-time judges may have been rather inefficient since they worked in the court sporadically; the low correlations shown in 1950 certainly suggest this. As this fact has become increasingly apparent, a policy shift by the Judicial Conference has occurred such that part-time judges have been gradually eliminated. As the formal policy states, this court shall develop "with a view toward creating and maintaining a system of full-time referees [judges]" (*U.S. Code Annotated, Title 28,* 1969, p. 21). Of course, one might also argue that the number of bankruptcies grew at such a rapid and unexpected rate that the shift to a full-time staff was essential and hence will continue to be necessary in the future— a position that the judges have in fact taken in the debates on court reform.

Each judge is formally assigned one nonjudicial staff person: however, additional personnel may be added if special permission is granted by the Administrative Office of the United States Courts. While this decision is not left to the judges themselves, it is nevertheless a simpler procedure than is the actual granting of an additional full-time or part-time judge slot. Therefore, enforcement of the formal rule of judicial-nonjudicial personnel relations may become the exceptional situation, particularly if demand for services increases.

While the clerks of the court are strongly associated with all measures of the task environment (with the exception of the average of the organizational matrix, $r = -.02$), the correlations shown with the court's caseload (pending, $r = .90$; filings, $r = .96$; demand, $r = .94$) are dramatic. (Note that data are available only for 1970.) That is, the size of the nonjudicial staff grows with the caseload of a court. As the court presently exists, nonjudicial staff do not have the authority to settle bankruptcy disputes; they may only prepare work for a judge who must ultimately decide the case. Yet it is apparent that judges certainly rely upon nonjudicial staff. The question then arises: can nonjudicial staff—civil servants—also make the final determination in a bankruptcy case if sufficient written and uniform guidelines are made available? Clearly, this is a possibility that is not in the best interests of judges but is nevertheless being suggested by some reformers. The fact that nonjudicial staff are so strongly associated with the workload of bankruptcy cases suggests that this may, in fact, be a realistic possibility.

Resources

The other side of the court's size is measured by its monetary resources. Since the selection process that determines the inclusion of full-time or part-time judges and of nonjudicial staff is essentially political, the second aspect of size (i.e., resources) becomes of critical importance. Resources of a court have been broken down into salaries paid to judges, both full-time and part-time, and salaries paid to the nonjudicial work force. The relative proportion of judicial to nonjudicial salaries further specifies the court's emphasis in responding to changing interorganizational demands. That is, it is important to know if the courts put greater emphasis on increasing the resources of nonjudicial personnel (to prepare the work for judicial personnel) or, if it finds such increases to be inadequate and instead demands that judicial personnel maintain control over the coordination of tasks within the organization. The juxtaposition of resources (or the monies of a court) and the number of personnel further specifies the relationship among the number of people assigned to the court, the actual monetary support they are given, and the relative support for judicial versus nonjudicial staff.

Table 5-2 also shows correlations between the caseload, casemix, organizational matrix, and judicial and nonjudicial resources of the bankruptcy court in 1970. (Note that data are available only for 1970.) Like the findings for personnel discussed above, judicial and nonjudicial resources are strongly associated with measures of the court's task environment. Again note that nonjudicial resources, like nonjudicial personnel, are particularly strongly associated with measures of the caseload of the court (pendings, $r = .88$; filings, $r = .95$; demand, $r = .93$); moreover, the total earnings of the organizational matrix shows a strong effect on judicial ($r = .87$) and nonjudicial ($r = .82$) resources. In contrast to personnel, consumer cases (Chapter XIII) show a moderate effect on both judicial ($r = .51$) and nonjudicial ($r = .57$) resources; these findings suggest that consumer cases are relatively expensive bankruptcy procedures that tend to require additional input from judicial and nonjudicial personnel once a district, or a judge, has made an informal policy decision to encourage this procedure (see chapter 3).

It is also necessary to consider the relative importance of these variables in influencing the size of the court. To that end, the relative effects of task structure variables and organizational matrix measures have been analyzed separately (table 5-3 and 5-4) and in combination (table 5-5).

Table 5-3
Zero-Order Correlations (r), Standardized Regression Coefficients ($b*$), and Squared Multiple Correlation Coefficients (R^2) for Four Categories of Task on the Personnel and Resources of the Bankruptcy Court in 1950, 1960, and 1970.

Task		Personnel							Resources	
		Full-time Judges			Part-time Judges			Clerks	Judicial	Nonjudicial
		'50	'60	'70	'50	'60	'70	'70	'70	'70
Caseload										
Filings	r	−.05	.63	.87	.11	−.01	−.16	.96	.88	.95
	$b*$	−.02	.38	.49	.12	.17	−.32	.75	.47	.83
Casemix										
Asset	r	.78	.61	.75	.24	−.11	.09	.75	.76	.71
	$b*$	.63	.25	.20	.51	−.23	.14	.07	.22	–
Business	r	.73	.50	.75	.12	−.04	−.19	.71	.75	.69
	$b*$	.18	.29	.37	−.32	−.01	−.12	.24	.37	.21
Consumer	r	.25	.08	.49	.07	−.06	.02	.58	.51	.57
	$b*$	.24	–	.03	.09	−.11	.20	.03	.06	.01
	R^2	.69	.53	.87	.10	.03	.06	.96	.88	.93

The Task Structure and Size of the Bankruptcy Court

Table 5-3 shows the separate ($b*$) and joint (R^2) effects of selected task variables (filings, asset, business, and consumer cases) with measures of personnel and resources in 1950, 1960, and 1970.[1] Full-time judges are the central pillars of this court. Table 5-3 shows that the joint effect for all four task structure variables increases from 1950 to 1970. By 1970, the combined effect of the court's caseload and casemix explains over three-fourths (R^2 = .87) of the variance in the number of full-time judges; this represents a rather significant increase from 1950 (R^2 = .69) and 1960 (R^2 = .53). It was shown above that the caseload (e.g. pending, filings, and demand) of the court revealed a stronger simple correlation with the number of full-time judges through time. A comparison of the standardized regression coefficients for each of the independent variables with full-time judges essentially confirms this analysis: whereas in 1950, asset cases were the main effect ($b*$ = .63) in and explanation of judges, by 1970, both filings ($b*$ = .49) and business cases ($b*$ = .37) contributed to the joint effect. In sum, the growth of the full-time judicial staff is clearly explained by the simultaneous growth in the court's workload.

By contrast, however, the part-time judicial staff is not explained by these factors. This is in part due to the policy of the court, with its clear push in the direction of a full-time staff. As the previous analyses have also shown, the part-time judge is a peripheral figure in this organization.

Nonjudicial clerks are, like full-time judges, explained by the task structure of the court (R^2 = .96). However, unlike full-time judges, bankruptcy filings are the main effect ($b*$ = .75) in an explanation of such cases. This means that the gross workload of the court is relatively the most important variable to consider in an explanation of nonjudicial workers. Since most filings are actually consumer cases (see chapter 3), these findings suggest that the nonjudicial staff of the court is primarily associated with consumer cases. By contrast, of course, full-time judges are also explained by business-type cases.

What is the relative effect of the court's caseload and casemix on judicial and nonjudicial resources? Table 5-3 also shows the results of the multiple and partial regression analysis of the court's task structure with resources—judicial and nonjudicial—for 1970. The combined effect of the court's caseload and casemix explains well over three-fourths of the variance of both judicial (R^2 = .88) and nonjudicial (R^2 = .93) resources. Yet a comparison of the standardized regression coefficients reveals that the sources of these combined effects are rather different. The direct effect of filings ($b*$ = .47), asset ($b*$ = .22), and business ($b*$ = .37) cases each contributes to the explained variance of judicial resources. By contrast, filings ($b*$ = .83) are the main effect in an explanation of nonjudicial resources. It appears, then, that judicial resources grow in response to both the volume and complexity of work in a court; more particularly, judicial resources are associated with complex—i.e., business—cases.

However, nonjudicial resources are essentially a response to the volume of cases that come before the court. Thus, judicial resources complement business cases whereas nonjudicial resources complement what are basically consumer cases. Certainly the results of the analysis of the personnel of the court also suggest this conclusion. This raises an interesting question: are nonjudicial workers presently administering consumer bankruptcies, thus leaving the judges free to adjudicate more complex, "important," and perhaps challenging, business cases? The findings do rather persuasively suggest this.

The Organizational Matrix and Size of the Bankruptcy Court

Table 5-4 shows the results of the multiple and partial regression analysis of measures of the organizational matrix with personnel and resources. Again, the presence of part-time judges is not explained by the organizational matrix of this court.

However, the total earnings of the organizational matrix shows a greater effect on full-time judges from 1950 to 1970. Likewise, the organizational matrix also appears to be a critical variable in an explanation of nonjudicial clerks as well as judicial and nonjudicial resources. Two points are now apparent: developments in the court's environment have had a dramatic effect upon the formation of a cohesive matrix of middle-class professionals (see chapter 4) who in turn depend upon this court for a livelihood. However, this matrix has also affected the actual development of this court, as seen in an explanation of its personnel and resources.

Official policy states that staff shall be added in response to the "conditions" of local communities. Since the federal courts are a decentralized network of organizations (Richardson and Vines 1970), policy decisions concerning personnel and resources allocations are made in Washington, but with input from local groups—e.g. judges, bar associations, unions, and so on (*U.S. Code, Annotated Title 11, Section 68,* 1971). The conditions and needs of lawyers and trustees are, these findings suggest, clearly part of the calculus that the Judicial Conference has considered in the development of this court. There may be a time lag between these requests and allocations for additional support; however, in spite of this possible delay factor, these groups seem to have developed clearly articulated political communications between local districts and Washington that may be quite effective in their present organization.

In light of the findings shown in tables 5-3 and 5-4, which factor of the court's task environment has been relatively the most important?

Table 5-4
Zero-Order Correlations (r), Standardized Regression Coefficients (b^*), and Squared Multiple Correlation Coefficients (R^2) for the Organizational Matrix on the Personnel and Resources of the Bankruptcy Court in 1950, 1960, and 1970

| | Personnel | | | | | | | Resources | |
| | Full-time Judges | | | Part-time Judges | | | Clerks | Judicial | Nonjudicial |
	'50	'60	'70	'50	'60	'70	'70	'70	'70
Organizational matrix									
Total									
r	.56	.69	.87	.13	−.09	−.18	.85	.87	.82
b^*	.62	.70	.92	.10	−.09	−.21	.94	.92	.90
Average									
r	−.06	−.15	.11	.10	.03	.05	−.02	.11	−.04
b^*	−.23	−.17	−.16	.07	.04	.11	−.29	−.16	−.30
R^2	.36	.51	.78	.02	.01	.04	.80	.79	.75

From 1950 to 1970: The Task Structure, Organizational Matrix,
and Size of the Bankruptcy Court

The research strategy in the preceeding section analyzed the impact of the task structure and the organizational matrix on the size (personnel and resources) of the bankruptcy court. As early as 1950, the organizational matrix was an important variable in an explanation of the court's size. The process of reform may present the opportunity to formally define and incorporate this matrix of personnel into the bankruptcy court. However, the impact of the task structure from 1950 to 1970 has also been significant.

Table 5-5 shows the direct, separate, and joint effects of the total earnings of the organizational matrix and bankruptcy filings on the number of full-time judges in 1950, 1960, and 1970. The joint effect of these independent variables has increased dramatically from 1950 (R^2 = .32) to 1970 (R^2 = .86); thus, by 1970 the variables of the bankruptcy court's task environment explain well over three-fourths of the variance in the number of full-time judges. In theory, the task environment specifies the relationship between inter- and intra-organizational variables; however, the practices of this court, i.e., the activities of bankruptcy adjudication, have blurred this distinction. The blurring of this organizational distinction also has important political consequences. Legally, lawyers who work in this court are privately employed; yet, the dramatic impact of this legal community upon the court suggests that they nevertheless have affected the direction of this organization. In sum, the relationship between the "private" bankruptcy bar and the court may more accurately be described

Table 5-5
Zero-Order Correlations (r), Standardized Regression
Coefficients (b^*), and Multiple Correlation Coefficients (R^2)
for the Tasks and Organizational Matrix on Personnel of the
Bankruptcy Court in 1950, 1960, and 1970

		Full-time Judges		
		'50	'60	'70
Filings	r	−.05	.63	.87
	b^*	−.05	.22	.49
Organizational matrix	r	.56	.69	.87
	b^*	.56	.52	.49
	R^2	.32	.50	.86

as a "bureaucratic chain" from lawyer to trustee to judge—a development that has also been documented in criminal courts (Blumberg 1970).

A comparison of the respective standardized regression coefficients at each point in time further specifies the relative impact of these variables on the organizational structure of the court. In 1950, the organizational matrix was the main effect ($b* = .56$) in an explanation of judges; by 1970, however, both the organizational matrix ($b* = .49$) and filings ($b* = .49$) contributed equally to the explained variance of full-time judges. On the face of it, this suggests that lawyers and trustees have lost influence in this court; however, upon closer examination the picture is actually more complicated. First of all, the simple correlation between filings and judges increased dramatically from 1950 ($r = -.05$) when it was insignificant to 1970 ($r = .87$) when it was strong; hence, the direct effect in 1950 ($b* = -.05$) and 1970 ($b* = .49$) also reflects this historical transition. Likewise, the simple correlation between the organizational matrix and judges in 1950 ($r = .56$) and 1970 ($r = .87$) has also increased dramatically. By 1970, then, these findings suggest, both task-oriented considerations and informal political liaisons were effecting the development and future of this court. It is actually not clear if this matrix of professionals has lost influence, or if this court's caseload demands have become so great that they can no longer be ignored—a conflict that also characterizes the political process of reform.

The Professional versus the Bureaucratic Alternative

The increased reliance upon specialized professional personnel and the increased use of administrators to coordinate tasks are not, by definition, antithetical alternatives in the history of organization. Research in organizational settings suggests that as professionals become increasingly specialized, or expert, in narrowly defined areas of work, administrative coordination becomes an increasingly common solution (Heydebrand 1973b; Edwards 1972, 1975; Gintis 1976; Marglin 1974). Yet the organizational arrangement of this court complements a generalist professional model without the support of an administrative staff.

Weber's work on law suggests that the implementation of law, as an aspect of domination, is, by definition, carried out by demarcated strata specifically trained in the area. The formation of the bankruptcy court reveals that within that context, areas of the law can be further specified into limited areas of expertise. The paradox of specialized professionals in a generalist work context is a core issue in the debates over court reform and reflects a frequently cited tension in professional organizations (Meyer 1972). Moreover, this tension magnifies the fact that the hierarchical bureaucratic solution for organizational change is not the only one, but rather one alternative: "The power position of bureaucracy cannot be decided *a priori* by its indispensability or its other characteristics" (Mouzelis 1972, p. 25). In the case examined here, the bureaucratic alternative is exemplified by the reform proposal to establish an administrative agency housed in the executive branch of government. However equally important is the professional alternative exemplified by the proposal to reform the court into a fully judicial and autonomous court structure. Thus, the Judges' Bill suggests a professional alternative by improving the court's status as an autonomous organization to adjudicate bankruptcy cases. The Commission's Bill suggests that the bankruptcy court should become an administrative agency housed in the executive branch of government and, in so doing, minimize its reliance upon a professional staff.

As this court continues to tax the resources of the state (see table 5-1) the bureaucratic alternative, through the extended use of nonjudicial personnel, directly meets the political cry for efficiency and rationality. Yet this alternative also changes the nature of the organization through the introduction of a formal division of labor, written rules, and delegation of responsibilities (Weber 1946a). Thus, bureaucratic administration challenges both traditional judicial authority and, by extension, the ideology of due process, "rule of law," and the adversary system itself (Heydebrand 1976; Wolff 1968). As these debates reveal, the judges use this point to support their bill, the professional alternative.

The issue of professionalization versus bureaucratization of the court goes to the heart of this debate. Interest groups who speak to this issue include lawyers, creditors, legal scholars, consumer law advocates, and U.S. Attorneys. Consideration will be given first to those interest groups that support the Commission's Bill, or the bureaucratic alternative, and then those who support the Judges' Bill, or the professional alternative.

The Bureaucratic Alternative

Legal Scholars: Legal scholars set the stage for this debate by raising Constitutional issues. They argue that presently judges in bankruptcy assume numerous administrative responsibilities, such as the appointment of trustees and auctioneers. Organizationally, such responsibilities are a waste of highly trained judicial time. Legally, such responsibilities establish a conflict of interest by minimizing the necessary impartiality of the judge. This, one legal scholar argues that

it is . . . the almost unanimous opinion of those who work in the field . . . that the bankruptcy courts should be relieved of the many administrative chores they now perform in the administration of the Bankruptcy Act so that they can come to their judging tasks free from *ex parte* contacts with the trustee and parties in interest and free from opinions and judgements based on the processing of papers which would not be admissible as evidence in the cases before them as judge. (*House Hearings* 1975, pp. 343-44)

From the perspective of legal scholars, it is necessary to sever absolutely judicial and bureaucratic responsibilities by removing such administrative aspects of bankruptcy from both the court and the Bankruptcy Division of the Administrative Office of the U.S. Courts.

Political dialogue by legal scholars also includes criticism of the Judges' Bill: "The 'judges' bill' adopts a number of the substantive reforms which the Commission proposed, but their structural proposals are not reforms. Instead, they seem intended mainly to enhance the functions and status of the former bankruptcy [judges]" (*House Hearings* 1975, p. 362; also see *Senate Hearings* 1975, pp. 870-80). Or, as another legal scholar put the matter, "I think the Judges' Bill is the result of the fact that these are judges and they want to be judges and judges' judges and this accounts for what is the Judges' Bill, the need for status" (*House Hearings* 1976, p. 869).

At the same time, some legal scholars also challenge the Commission's Bill, stating that it is necessary to implement a structure that will meet the needs of the majority of bankrupts. Thereby all cases, except corporate and railroad reorganization, should fall under the auspices of an agency that has administrative law judges to handle controversies on the spot. Some legal scholars even go on to argue that to delay justice by separating these agencies is ultimately detrimental to the client (*House Hearings* 1975, p. 364).

Thus, legal experts have taken a position that defines the fundamental problem (i.e., the overlap between adjudicatory and administrative responsibilities), support one of the alternative solutions, (i.e., administrative law judges), and criticizes other solutions (i.e., The Judges' Bill). Experts give strength to the debate by introducing a position in legal terms. The implied political position rests upon a scholarly understanding of the law and its guidelines.

Consumer Groups: Consumer advocates pose the question of a professional or bureaucratic alternative in yet another way. They tend to argue that if the statutes are fair and equitable, it makes little difference where the case is heard. Consumer advocates support an organization that guarantees a separation of the above functions and incorporates educational services. Where this is done is not important: "From the consumer perspective, there is no magic to one type of forum or another. The important consideration is that the forum afford due process in both the legal and equitable meaning of the term" (*Senate Hearings* 1975, p. 307). By presenting their position in these terms, consumer advocates emphasize a crucial aspect of their concerns—a redefinition of the court's tasks. But, some do not see a connection between the nature of the organization and the task structure itself. Like legal scholars, consumer advocates argue that the crucial challenge is to provide a forum in which the "separation of the gathering of sensitive client information from the process which considers and determines the disposition of consumer cases" is guaranteed (*Senate Hearings* 1975, p. 307).

A consequence of being outsiders to this court's history is that various consumer advocates address different issues; that is, they are without the "team" support that creditors, lawyers, and judges share. In fact, it is perhaps more accurate to refer to the consumer advocates as various individual, rather than group, voices. Hence, whereas one advocate does not directly address the impact of a bureaucratic alternative for reform, another does: "To the extent that a separate administrative body in bankruptcy would reduce administrative costs, establish confidence in the system by the public and create sorely needed uniformity, I favor the establishment of the Bankruptcy Administration" (*House Hearings* 1976, p. 1339). Moreover, perhaps the most radical argument is heard when this same spokesperson goes on to argue that

The more affluent person who has financial difficulties will have the benefit of pre-filing counseling and preparation by consulting with an attorney, whereas the segment of our population less advantaged economically will not seek the advice of a qualified practitioneer because they may be lulled into beliving that it may be necessary. (*House Hearings* 1976, p. 1340)

Yet, this position is not to be confused with that of judges or lawyers, for example. The context of this advocate's position reveals that he is posing a fundamental challenge of "bureaucratic due process," i.e., the "filtering" mechanism of an administrative agency whereby only the "controversial," the important (i.e., business) cases surface for judicial review.

U.S. Attorney's Office: In part, the U.S. Attorney's Office represents the executive branch. Couched in terms that support the position of legal scholars—that administrative and judicial functions should be separate—the representative of the U.S. Attorney's Office carries the logic of this argument one step further and supports part of the Judges' Bill:

The time is also ripe for administrative innovations to computerize accounting, disbursement and statistical reporting functions to achieve the economies and efficiencies which the public has a right to expect of the bankruptcy system . . . . We believe it is desirable to test the use of an enlarged role of the Administrative Office of the U.S. Courts as the bankruptcy judges propose, to see what results and economies can be obtained. If these results and economies do not meet expectations, further study can then be given to the proposal of a separate Bankruptcy Administration in the Executive Branch. (*Senate Hearings* 1975, p. 476; also see *House Hearings* 1976, p. 2099)

While the representative of the U.S. Attorney's Office presents a position that is a departure from a traditionally adjudicatory model, it is proposed as a test case.

It is the clear-cut reliance upon computerization, as against bureaucratization, that provides the organizing principle of this position.

The argument by the representative of the U.S. Attorney's Office raises an important question: is it possible to circumvent the rational bureaucratic model (i.e., formal rules, hierarchy, and officials) that Weber suggests is the logical organizational development in a western society? Is it surprising that a technological solution (i.e., computers) is supported by "old" professionals (i.e., lawyers)? The possibility of technological coordination through the introduction of computers suggests that hierarchical, bureaucratic coordination is a historically specific example of organizational development. That is, hierarchical bureaucratic coordination may represent an older organizational form. The introduction of technological coordination, in a professional work context, may emerge as a "compromise" alternative during court reform.

Business Creditors: Business creditors support a clear distinction between a forum for business cases and a forum for consumer cases. That is, they have more to gain from an organization that handles only business cases. Creditors benefit from the present structure of the court through its business caseload. Credit managers, as represented by their association, base their position on the demands of the task structure and, consequently, support a modified administrative agency:

The Association recommends that the function of such an office be limited to *consumer* cases. In the commercial field, creditors are sufficiently sophisticated and motivated to direct the administration of such cases. The Association also supports the provision in the Judges' Bill providing that the office be established in the Judicial Branch lest there be an "empire-building" executive agency. (*Senate Hearings* 1975, p. 433; also see *House Hearings* 1976, pp. 1666-74)

Support for a bureaucratic alternative is based upon different rationales. Legal scholars base their argument on the adjudicatory role of a judge. Consumer advocates argue that the structure of the forum is a secondary question. The creditors' position is based upon an understanding of where their most lucrative cases lie. Finally, the U.S. Attorney supports the introduction of computers as another alternative.

The Professional Alternative

Judges. Different groups support professionalization in various ways. Clearly, the group that is in most direct support of this alternative are the judges themselves. The suggestion that bankruptcy law, as a legal procedure, has come of age and thus warrants its own autonomous organization epitomizes the position of the judges. Their position is a direct challenge to the Commission.

Thus, it is important to understand how they justify that challenge. The rationale of the judges' position rests upon the importance of considering the quality of justice as well as its organizational housing. Thus, the judges argue that the Commission staff has been drawn from the business bankruptcy community and has ignored the problem of consumer bankruptcy. They argue that judges in bankruptcy are the only knowledgeable group with first-hand information on the importance of the quality of justice that a court of law must seek to preserve. Moreover, the judges' position is couched in terms that support the fundamental challenge of the present structure—the overlap between administrative and adjudicatory functions. Thus, a judge argues that

[the Judges' Bill] tries to preserve a court-oriented delivery system. The case is to be filed with the *bankruptcy court* clerk. Basic control of the case would remain with the court, which has the responsibility for its judicial effectiveness. To free the judicial function, the Judges' Bill delegates administrative duties to an expanded version of the existing Bankruptcy Division of the administrative office, within the judicial branch of government. (*House Hearings* 1975, p. 510)

The Commission argues that the court has produced a group of "rings and cliques" that control the court. On this point, the judges meet the challenge by arguing that "the practical fact of the matter is that, if specialization in bankruptcy practice and administration is what is meant by a 'bankruptcy ring' then that is exactly what is needed" (*Senate Hearings* 1975, p. 76). The judges first establish their credibility by emphasizing their expertise. Next, they support the fundamental challenge to the present structure, the overlap between adjudicatory and administrative responsibilities. Finally, they turn the alleged rings and cliques of the court into an attribute of the structure that ultimately benefits the bankrupt party. With these carefully laid arguments to meet any challenges, the judges then demonstrate why the Judges' Bill, which supports the professional route for this court, is superior.

Reform must upgrade the court so as to attract good people to work in this area. In fact, the Judges' Bill will do more to attract such people than will an increase in salaries. One way to upgrade this court is to separate the bankruptcy court from the district court: "To maintain a stable cadre of bankruptcy judges and to provide necessary authority for all who man the bankruptcy bench, this court should be, in our judgment, made fully independent and strengthened in the process. The divorce from the district court should be clean and complete" (*House Hearings* 1975, p. 513). So, separation from the district court upgrades the court, attracting better people who, in turn, will better serve the clients of the court. Professionalization of the bankruptcy court, as suggested in the Judges' Bill, involves the establishment of a fully autonomous organization. The organizational demand of reporting to the district court is "semibureaucratic." The judges are using the process of court reform to establish a clean and complete separation from the district court and, in so doing, sever their "bureaucratic" (i.e., hierarchical) relationship with the district court.

But the Commission's Bill seeks to remove the major work in bankruptcy from the judiciary and place it in the executive. To this, the judges reply that

if the apparatus is retained in the judicial branch, if it is built on the existing Bankruptcy Division . . . the long-standing constitutional tradition of separation of powers would thereby be observed; . . . *more importantly, all persons with claims of relief, irrespective of the dollars involved, would have free, direct and immediate access to an independent court.* (*House Hearings* 1975, p. 513, emphasis added)

The judges' position is based upon the need to preserve an adjudicatory forum for all potential clients, consumer or business. In essence, judges seek to show that the Commission's Bill, through bureaucratization, assumes that the important reason for changing the structure is that the court primarily handles simple cases. Echoing a pluralist ideology, the judges argue that no bankruptcy case should be denied a prestigious forum.

The judges also argue that the administrator, under the proposed system, would be both arbitrator and administrator, thus undermining the fundamental reason for change. That is, according to the judges, the Commission's Bill ultimately combines all aspects of bankruptcy procedure:

The Administrator would be authorized and at various times required to serve as *judge, litigant, counselor* to debtors, *advisor* and *consultant* to creditors, *appointer* of fiduciaries, *clerk* of the court, *trustee, receiver, distributing agent, court advisor, liquidator, appraiser, rulemaker* and *regulator* of fees, as well as the head of an independent federal agency within the Executive Branch of Government. *The Commission suggestion is not so much that we should "throw the baby out with the bathwater," as it is that he be thrown out without a bath, in preference for one whose more conspicuous birthmarks are impervious to bathwater.* (*Senate Hearings* 1975, p. 85)

Finally, the professionalization of the bankruptcy court must involve a change in the appeals procedure. Following the logic of the judges' position, the bankruptcy court should be upgraded to the same level as the United States Federal District Court (*House Hearings* 1976, pp. 2663-64). Appeals should go to a higher court, the circuit court, rather than a court of coequal authority, the district court. The appeals structure that the judges support is the most explicit statement of their attempt to professionalize this organization. To support their position, they argue that

we are convinced that no useful purpose can be served by having appeals from the decisions of a trial court specializing in bankruptcy jurisdiction proceed to a coequal court of general jurisdiction. Not only is the district court not really equipped and designed to function as an appellate tribunal, it will no longer be sufficiently involved, under the new proposals, in bankruptcy proceedings to warrant its establishment as the higher or appellate court of bankruptcy. (*Senate Hearings* 1975, p. 55)

The judges not only challenge the alternative presented by the Commission, they also present their case for fundamentally upgrading the traditionally parajudicial, or semibureaucratic, relationship between the district court and the bankruptcy court.

Mannheim (1936) suggests that bureaucrats seek to turn problems of politics into problems of administraion. Bendix and Roth take that point one step further by suggesting that "professionals tend to turn every problem of decision-making into a question of expertise" (1971, p. 148). It is not surprising that bankruptcy judges rest their cases on expertise in this area as a tactic to legitimate a political position. After all, they rest their case for the professional alternative for bankruptcy court on their day-to-day "pragmatic" knowledge, which has given them, they claim, an expertise superior to that of all other groups.

The judges have significant and important supporters for their position. They include the representative of the present Bankruptcy Division of The Administrative Office of the United States Court, bankers, and creditors.[2]

Bankruptcy Division. The representative of the Bankruptcy Division of the Administrative Office supports the judges' position by arguing that the bankruptcy court handles legal problems and not "social problems." "Counseling," therefore, has no place in the adjudication of cases. Implicit in this argument is criticism of the consumer law advocates and the Commission (*House Hearings* 1975, pp. 3-12). By attacking this issue, the representative of the Bankruptcy Division presents an issue in support of the judges that the judges themselves did not touch upon directly.

The representative of the Bankruptcy Division also supports the introduction of computerization:

The real strength of the recommended legislation is found in the mandate to adopt modern business techniques, such as computerization, to the bankruptcy process. In my estimation, the implementation of this mandate, plus improvement in the substantive laws in conjunction with clarified procedures under the Rules of Bankruptcy Procedure, is the essence of the improvement we will see in the system. (*House Hearings* 1975, p. 5; also see *Senate Hearings* 1975, pp. 897-905)

According to the representative of the Bankruptcy Division, the introduction of computer technology and business techniques is the way to improve the structure of the court within an adjudicatory organizational structure. In other words, the representative of the Bankruptcy Division supports the judges but relies upon different issues to make the case. The case that this representative selects to discuss was also supported by the representative of the U.S. Attorney's Office. Besides the judges, the representative of the Bankruptcy Division is the most direct advocate of the Judges' Bill. Discussion of computerization, under the rubric of general support for the Judges' Bill, again supports a point made earlier: it appears that technological coordination may emerge as a significant direction for reform of the bankruptcy court.

Consumer Creditors. The creditors who support the Judges' Bill do not take issue with the fact that adjudicatory and administrative functions must be separated. However, they go on to argue that the separation of such functions does not necessarily mean that all aspects of bankruptcy procedure should be turned over to civil servants (*Senate Hearings* 1975, p. 535; also see *House Hearings* 1976, pp. 542-52). The very status of a civil servant suggests that the bankrupt party would not receive adequate legal advice, making it almost impossible for the client to be assured of an equitable forum (*Senate Hearings* 1975, p. 213; also see *House Hearings* 1976, pp. 897-908). Like the judges, consumer creditors take the position that the bankruptcy court needs to be accorded respect and authority analogous to that of the district court (*House Hearings* 1976, p. 1044). They argue that the bankruptcy court will not attract qualified judges until the system is upgraded and the pay scale is increased. (Also see *House Hearings* 1976, pp. 1747-74.) Finally, the most direct support for the judges' position is heard when creditors argue that "the suggestion that the same agency which undertakes the adjudication, administration, supervision and trusteeship of the estate of a bankrupt should also serve as counsel for the bankrupt, whether such person be a lay person or a duly licensed attorney, is fraught with patent and irreconcilable conflicts" (*Senate Hearings* 1975, p. 193). Whereas creditors who primarily work within the business sector support two separate structures, drawn along consumer-business lines, creditors who work within the consumer sector support the professionalization of the court through steps suggested in the Judges' Bill. These differing positions by groups who work in the same area, but with different clients, suggest that the development of the bankruptcy court has led to the stratification of the organizational matrix due to the increasingly varied caseload of the court. Those creditors who have a less lucrative clientele (i.e., consumers) seek to improve their standing through professionalization.

The difference of position among creditors on the issue of a professional or bureaucratic alternative supports the findings of chapter 3, that the changing dynamics of the court's environment have produced a more differentiated set of tasks, a distinctly consumer-based set of tasks, and a distinctly business-based set of tasks. The distinction between such tasks has resulted in two bankruptcy courts in its informal, if not its formal, structure. Creditors who enter the political arena to debate court reform also reflect the informal structure of the court. These debates on court reform demonstrate that the political needs of consumer creditors and business creditors are antithetical. While business debtors may not have a "direct" advocate in the process of court reform, it is clear that they, as a group, have their needs articulated.

Bankers. Those interested in banking who address reform are more concerned with consumer than with business cases. Thus, their support for the professional alternative for this court through the Judges' Bill is not surprising. They argue that the establishment of a Bankruptcy Administration, housed in the executive, is objectionable on a number of grounds. Their arguments are familiar by now:

It strains trust in human nature to the breaking point to believe that an administrative office can (i) counsel the debtor as to available reliefs, (ii) serve as trustee, and (iii) then fairly deal with a secured creditor at a valuation hearing (where as adverse determination might suggest that the advice given under (i) was incorrect). We are not comforted by the argument that different personnel in the administrative office might be serving different functions. (*House Hearings* 1976, p. 1023; also see *Senate Hearings* 1975, pp. 124–31)

Bankers speak directly to the question of removal of the trustee (the individual in the present structure who oversees the creditors in a case) as suggested by the Commission and argue that it is preferable to maintain a panel of trustees within the court. They go on to argue that legal counseling should not be undertaken by an administrator, but rather by a lawyer, that the bankruptcy court should maintain a panel of lawyers who work in this area, and that the Judges' Bill "preserves the confidential relationship of the attorney and the client" (*Senate Hearings* 1975, p. 126). Finally, bankers claim that bankruptcy should remain under the auspices of the judicial branch of government.

   Bankers and consumer creditors explicitly support the Judges' Bill and rest their case with the services demanded by consumer bankruptcy cases. It is unclear why the consumer absolutely needs a lawyer; however, it is clear why creditors need a trustee and, therefore, support the professional alternative. Consumer creditors implicitly see their interests being better served by a court that is an extension of the present set of relationships.

Practicing Attorneys. The last group that we must consider is attorneys. Lawyers tend to support the maintenance of a status quo. Stated in its simplest terms, one lawyer responded under questioning, "Your bankruptcy bar is going to go into another area of practice, because there is no room left for them in the Commission Bill" (*Senate Hearings* 1975, p. 176). The entire thrust of the Commission's Bill, with its emphasis upon bureaucratization, will discourage lawyers from participating in this area of practice. The bureau-cratization of bankruptcy procedure removes lawyers from the litigation process. As another lawyer argues,

inefficiencies are always a source of difficulty in any government system. We submit that the solution of these problems can best be achieved within the framework of the existing system. The present system is quite efficient. The overall cost to debtors is less than any other recognized method of extended payment of debt. (*Senate Hearings* 1975, pp. 579-80)

The arguments posed by these attorneys echo those of the judges them-selves: administration "offends one's concept of due process" (*Senate Hearings* 1975, p. 400; also see *House Hearings* 1976, pp. 731-55); the "upgrading" of this court is more important than increasing salary levels (*Senate Hearings* 1975, p. 956; also see *House Hearings* 1976, p. 1538); and, appeals should proceed to the circuit court, not the district court (*Senate Hearings* 1975, p. 1539).

Finally, in the lawyers' view, the Commission's proposed system not only confuses the functions that are delegated to the administrator, but also has a built-in shortcoming that creates a greater possibility for controversy (i.e., adjudication) within a structure that will have fewer judges and fewer lawyers. They argue that this system will add delay and unreasonable expense to com-mercial and business bankruptcies. Lawyers, like creditors and the representa-tive of the Bankruptcy Division, suggest that the attempt to reduce cost and delay, as suggested by the Commission, will have the unanticipated effect of increasing both cost and delay.

Conclusion: The Rationalization of Collegial Organization

The reform of the bankruptcy court epitomizes a legal, professional organiza-tion caught between the principle of adjudication and the heavy demand to administer cases.

The analysis of these alternative solutions for organizing the activities of bankruptcy shows that court reform is beset by conflict. The conflict in this case arises from the fact that the various groups are not equally served by both proposals. In presenting a position for one or the other of these reforms, these groups must demonstrate its advantage not only for themselves, but also for the potential debtor. Those who support the Commission's Bill are, for the most part, outside the structure of the court; however, those who sup-port the Judges' Bill are from inside the structure of the court. Thus, this latter group has more to lose if their position—the professional solution—is not sup-ported by the Congress. From the judges' perspective, this professional transformation would establish a more autonomous structure for the activities of bankruptcy law and would thus redefine the status and increase the opportunities for mobility of those members of the legal community who have been part of this organization's development (see Thompson 1967). Reform, therefore, may have little to do with creating a more equitable and rational organization.

Concommitant with the historical forces that press toward the rationalization of law are historical forces that push toward the structural transformation of the collegial elements within a court. There are macro-historical trends particular to the western experience that shape the environment of monocratic rational bureaucratization.[3] These trends, in many respects, overlap and complement the rationalization of the law, the knowledge base of a court.

The market, and specifically the development of taxation, is according to Weber the first historical aspect of the causal nexus of legal-rational bureaucracy. The peculiar nature of the economic basis of modern society demands that calculability of results be possible. The development of a money economy rationalizes economic transaction and this specifically affects the form of bureaucracy insofar as the official is remunerated for specific services (i.e., knowledge) rendered.

Closely linked to the development of a money economy is the enlarged role of the state, and, specifically, the problem of communication: the demands of a sophisticated, modern mode of communication undermine collegial administration insofar as the need for "quick and unambiguous decisions . . . push to the fore" (Weber 1946a, p. 238). Only a bureaucratic structure is capable of handling the quantitatively increased and qualitatively changed demands of the state.

The history of modern bureaucracy parallels the history of mass democracy. The rise of mass democracy, with an emphasis upon equality before the law, lays the foundation for complex state structures and communications networks and therefore gives rise to the need for a rational administrative form that itself supports and legitimates the values of the equality of law and the availability of office.[4]

The rise of mass democracy, with its pull toward bureaucratic organization, is seen also in the formation of the legal theory of "administrative due process" that argues for an administrative system of laws and rules. Of course, such a theory contradicts the historically broad scope of judicial discretion: "From this perspective, the key to more responsible decision-making lies not in the judicialization of the administrative process, but rather in the bureaucratization of the judicial process" (Schubert 1960, p. 197; but see Nonet 1969; Selznick 1969).

However, the technical superiority of rational bureaucracy, *in and of itself*, gives it its persistent quality. Legal rational bureaucracy is the most effective tool for coordinating large-scale tasks; therefore its model will be mirrored in all areas of social life. There is, in this sense a "unilinear construction . . . implied in Weber's idea of the bureaucratic trend" (Gerth and Mills 1946, p. 51). Once modern bureaucracy takes hold, traditional, and even charismatic, forms of leadership are ineffective against the forces of rationalization.

The thrust of the Weberian challenge demands that the pull toward rational bureaucratization be considered as a concrete historical possibility in the analysis of reform. That is, bureaucratization is one means of coordinating tasks and it must be considered when examining concrete organizational formations. However, Weber's larger challenge lies in its perhaps inevitable reification across all social spheres. Is bureaucratization an institution in and of itself rather than a means to solving the tasks of particular institutional problems?[5] But the degree to which rational organizational change is possible hinges upon the political position of key groups. In short, it is not accurate to refer to rationalization as both technically superior and politically neutral.

During the reform of the bankruptcy court the thrust toward rationality, as derived from both the knowledge base and the collegial structure of the court, is a critical issue. On the one hand, the examination of the formation and transformation of the court reveals the twentieth-century pull toward the "technical" superiority of rational administration that all organizations confront. But on the other hand, this examination also reveals the historical roots of the legal community's control of adjudication and the parameters that this critical factor places upon the possibilities for reform.

Notes

1. Multicollinearity among the independent variables is again a problem. (In chapters 3 and 4 the problem of multicollinearity was handled through the use of factor scores and the selection of representative indicators; see appendix C.) In this case (see table 5-3) filings were selected to represent the "caseload" of the court since the correlations among filings, pending cases, and demand is high; see appendix D for the exact correlation among these indicators. See Blalock (1960) and Nie (1975) for a further discussion of various solutions to the problem of multicollinearity.

2. Some creditors supported the Commission's Bill in part. In other words, this group does not form a cohesive or unified voice. It seems that creditors of businesses and of consumers have very different political interests. Creditors of business find the organization of the court, which includes consumer cases, an unnecessary and time-consuming constraint. Creditors of consumers want to maintain an adversarial forum for settling their legal disputes.

3. The court is not irrational, but rather *less* rational than other organizational formations, for example the civil service.

4. This problem is discussed more specifically in Weber's analysis of natural law as a legitimating and revolutionary force: "The invocation of natural law has repeatedly been the method by which classes in revolt against the existing order have legitimated their aspirations, insofar as they did not, or could not, base their claims upon positive religious norms of relevation" (Weber 1954, p. 288).

5. Marx poses the question very differently. As Avineri points out, "the sociological significance of Marx's analysis of bureaucracy lies in his insistence that bureaucratic structures automatically reflect prevailing social power relations but pervert and disfigure them. Bureaucracy is the image of prevailing social power distorted by its claim to universality" (Avineri 1968, p. 51).

6

The Political and Social Meaning of Court Reform

Organizational effectiveness is perhaps the most complex question of this study. As commonly defined in the literature, effectiveness refers to the "degree to which a social system achieves its goals" (Price 1972, p. 101). The task structure is an analytic tool for examining what an organization does, regardless of the content of its stated goals (see chapter 3). But, the relative effectiveness of an organization considers both what the organization does and how closely it comes to achieving these stated goals. Seen in this light, effectiveness must be distinguished from efficiency. An organization may be efficient (e.g., highly productive) but ineffective in achieving its goal.

The stated goals of this court are to supervise those debtors (both individual and corporate) who have been unwilling to pay their debts, to rehabilitate debtors (both individual and corporate) by offering a "fresh start," and to provide an "orderly framework" in an open-credit economy for the control mechanism of the fresh start. While the legal options (see chapter 3) and the stated goals of the court are substantively similar for both individual and corporate cases, the degree of complexity of legal decisions, as well as the amount of money involved, differ depending upon whether a corporation or an individual is involved. The complexity of a bankruptcy proceeding is thus structured by the nature of the specific case (i.e., corporate versus consumer) rather than by the nature of the laws or rules that are drawn upon in determining the outcome.

However, these above considerations concerning organizational effectiveness assume a relative neutrality. That is, as presented in the literature, the closeness of "fit" between stated goals and achievement is a sufficient analytic concept. (See, e.g., Osborn and Hunt 1974; Seashore and Yuchtman 1967.)

The Politics of Organizational Effectiveness

But organizational effectiveness is also, and equally importantly, a political question: for whom is a social organization effective? This question implicitly raises ones of social class and structure—a classical issue of nineteenth-century social theory. Weber's work was concerned with understanding how a modernizing social structure can control the onslaught of rationalizing forces.

Given the historical configuration of the occidental experience, the

question arises: is there any way effectively to control this unilinear development such that its rational dimension does not, in fact, become irrational? As
Bendix points out, "the very conditions of efficiency that Weber specified also
can be the conditions that lead to a subversion of the rule of law and the transformation of bureaucracy from a policy implementing to a decision-making
body" (1962, p. 451). In other words, rational control can become the control
of things over persons.

Weber's discussion of effective control of bureaucratization is therefore,
in essence, a discussion of the control of domination. And this discussion com-
prises also a central issue of his political sociology. Throughout Weber's writings
on the subject of bureaucratization there is an underlying but clear argument
that rational, monocratic, bureaucratic control is a static phenomenon from the
point of view of the larger structural forces of political-economic life. Although
the internal mechanisms of specific organizations may be more or less rational,
the overarching dimensions of bureaucratic control are here to stay. Therefore,
when Weber speaks of "effective" control he assumes the viability of his perspective on bureaucratization; he does not consider the possibility of fundamental change in the political, social, and economic relations of the nation-state.
In Weber's view, it is not possible to overcome, to change fundamentally, a
society that fragments the world into seemingly unconnected and isolated
"projects."

Weber's perspective on bureaucracy is accompanied by an emphasis upon
individual responsibility and by an ethic of individual political action.[1]
Accepting the modern structure of legal-rational domination as a given, as an
inescapable outcome of modernization, the only viable solution then becomes
individual political responsibility that may be institutionalized through democratic control. Moreover, such democratic institutions demand political skills
that are antithetical to rational, technical, bureaucratic know-how.[2]

Weber begins with a political question. His solution, a working democracy,
ultimately rests upon control by selected strata or elites. Weber assumes that
administration in an industrialized society requires leadership that stands above
and outside of the bureaucratic structure: "Bureaucratic control has inevitably
at its apex an element which is not at least wholly rational" (Weber, as quoted
in Marcuse 1971, p. 147). Weber, however, does not devote his attention to
the question of whom this elite might represent in the larger society. "Effective control" of bureaucratic domination is static insofar as a class can never
control the state. Weber does not ask the question for whom this effective
control exists. Does control through "parliamentary democracy" imply a more
effective solution for the total citizenry? "Effectiveness and responsibility are
. . . not neutral dimensions of technical, formal rationality; they intrinsically
embody certain broad political orientations" (Wright 1974, pp. 101-102).
Weber considers unimportant the question of whether there are broad political
orientations that may benefit from effective control since effective political

control of rationalization may have significantly different meanings and implications in different political, social, and economic contexts.

The contribution of Weber's analysis is its demand for consideration of the political implications of bureaucratization and its control. However, Weber assumes that control of bureaucratization is both viable and beneficial for the total society. He does not consider the possibility of fundamental political, social, and economic change and the impact such change might have upon liberal democracy. More importantly, within the context of the democratic state, Weber omits from consideration the possibility that control of bureaucratization is more effective for particular class interests.

Organizational effectiveness is neither an isolated nor a neutral concept. Rather, it involves by definition an aspect of interorganizational analysis. Organizational effectiveness must examine the *political* relations between organizations by considering who benefits from those relations (Heydebrand 1973a, p. 59).

In looking at the issue of organizational effectiveness within the bankruptcy court is is necessary to consider both the degree to which this organization achieves its goals and the political implications of this organization's relative success.

A primary task of all courts is to dispose of cases in a relatively short period of time. It is a cliché within the law that justice delayed is justice denied. Thus, the first question in considering the organizational effectiveness of a court is that of the overall output. How many bankruptcy cases does the court actually dispose of?

Table 6-1 shows the total number of all bankruptcy terminations, the percentage terminated to filings, the percentage terminated to demand, and the percentage change from decade to decade since 1930. Clearly, the gross number of terminations has increased dramatically from 1930 (60,500) to 1970 (182,400). Moreover, the number of cases terminated increased by 188 percent from 1950 to 1960; though this value dropped rather significantly from 1960 to 1970 (84 percent), these figures do suggest that the work force of this court has been actively administering and adjudicating bankruptcy cases. Like the number of bankruptcy filings (see table 3-1a), by 1960 (99,300) the number of terminations exceeded that of 1930 (60,500), the early years of the Depression.

The percentage of terminations to filings shows that the personnel of the court have disposed of most of their workload each decade. There is a slight dip in 1950 (77 percent); but in any event the percentage of cases terminated is rather impressive.

Why is the cry raised to reform this court if most of the work is being completed within the present organization? As table 6-1 demonstrates, the percentage of terminations to demand reveals the problem. It will be recalled from chapter 3 that the pending cases of the docket are perhaps the most

Table 6-1
The Court's Organizational Effectiveness: 1930 to 1970

	Terminations	
1930	60,500	
1940	44,800	
1950	25,600	
1960	99,300	
1970	182,400	

	% of filings	*% of demand*
1930	96	49
1940	86	42
1950	77	40
1960	90	52
1970	94	49

	% Change
1930–1940	—26
1940–1950	—43
1950–1960	188
1960–1970	84

	Payment effectiveness creditors' claims	*% Paid*
1930	_a	_a
1940	_a	_a
1950	$ 21,400,000	22.0
1960	44,150,200	19.0
1970	489,400,000	17.0

[a]Not available.

important change in the court's caseload since 1950 (see tables 3-1a and 3-4). The figures shown in table 6-1 suggest that the backlog has the feedback effect of reducing the actual amount of work disposed of by the personnel of the court. That is, the personnel of this court are able to keep up with their work, but they are not able to get ahead; this predicament also describes, however, the larger federal district court (Heydebrand and Seron, forthcoming). But the relative share of work terminated has remained around 50 percent in 1930 and 1970, both when the judges of this court were primarily part-time and when they were primarily full-time. If backlog in terminations—congestion— is a rationale for reform, then it is not clear exactly why this is a more pressing problem today than it was twenty-five or thirty years ago. In sum, the figures shown in table 6-1 further suggest that the improved organizational effectiveness of this court may have little to do with the actual reasons for reform.

The bankruptcy court can be distinguished from other types of courts by its specialized task structure and by the demands that this type of task structure make on the organization. Regardless of the legal procedure taken, the "bankruptcy system seeks an equitable distribution among its creditors" (Shuchman 1971, p. 420). Of course the claims of creditors may not always coincide with the yield (in terms of payment) of a particular case. The relative congruence or discrepancy between claims and yields is a particularly important indicator of the court's stated effectiveness. "A fundamental goal of all true bankruptcy law is to provide for an equitable distribution of the debtors' assets through pro rata dividends to all creditors of the same class" (Cyr 1975, p. 168). This is referred to as payment effectiveness. How successful is the court in paying to creditors those claims made by creditors and approved by the court?

Table 6-1 shows also the claims of creditors and the percentage actually received in 1950, 1960, and 1970.[3] Whereas the amount of money claimed by creditors in bankruptcy cases has increased dramatically from 1950 ($21,400,000) to 1970 ($489,400,000), the percentage paid has remained approximately the same (1950, 22 percent; 1960, 19 percent; 1970, 17 percent). Moreover, the significant increase in claims occurred from 1960 to 1970 (100 percent). It will be recalled from chapter 3 that the definition of an asset case varies from state to state due to differing exemption laws; but in spite of this variation, the findings suggest that structural developments in the court's environment—i.e., competitive-sector manufacturing—may actually override these state-specific legal differences. That is, in 1970 competitive-sector measures, along with the number of government employees, accounted for the number of asset cases of a district. Though the number of asset cases, then, has remained relatively stable (table 3-1b), the environmental causes of such cases have changed. The significant increase in creditors' claims shown in table 6-1 also reflects this development: the bankruptcy court may not be hearing relatively more asset-type cases, in terms of gross numbers, but their relative complexity has increased rather dramatically over the decades. However, table 6-1 also suggests that the personnel of the court may not be any more successful in distributing these claims to creditors, in spite of an overall shift from a part-time to a full-time judicial staff.

The relationship between output and payment effectiveness specifies the relative degree of success the court has achieved in meeting its stated goal. However, both of these measures suggest that the court's success has not been outstanding. The question arises whether these factors of effectiveness are associated with and explained by the size (personnel and resources) of the bankruptcy court.

The Organizational Effectiveness of the Bankruptcy Court: 1950 to 1970

Table 6-2 shows zero-order correlations of personnel and resources with the terminations and payment effectiveness of the bankruptcy court in 1950, 1960, and 1970. It is clear from this table that part-time judges are not associated with terminations or payment effectiveness at all three points in time. As these personnel are not "explained" by the task environment (see table 5-5), so these judges do not contribute to the relative effectiveness of the court.

By contrast, the correlations between full-time judges and terminations have increased dramatically from 1950 ($r = .12$) to 1970 ($r = .87$). It was not until 1970 that the majority (85 percent) of judges in this court worked on a full-time basis. The significant increase, however, in the number of terminations occurred between 1950 and 1960 (188 percent). There is an inevitable time lag between new organizational demands and personnel or resource allocations, since all requests must be administered through Washington bureaucracies. Nevertheless, these findings suggest that the court disposed of more cases without the aid of a large full-time judicial staff. The question then arises: organizationally, is an autonomous, judicial staff actually necessary for the coordination and execution of bankruptcy matters?

While it is not possible to compare the effect of nonjudicial clerks across time, their effect in 1970 ($r = .97$) certainly suggests that they are a critical factor in the organization of this court. The relative allocation of judicial

Table 6-2
Zero-Order Correlations (Pearson's r) between the Effectiveness and the Personnel and Resources of the Bankruptcy Court in 1950, 1960, and 1970

| | *Organizational effectiveness* | | | | | |
| | *Terminations* | | | *Payment effectiveness* | | |
	'50	*'60*	*'70*	*'50*	*'60*	*'70*
Personnel						
Full-time judges	.12	.14	.87	−.02	.01	−.13
Part-time judges	.05	−.01	−.15	−.11	−.13	.11
Clerks	_[a]	_[a]	.97	_[a]	_[a]	−.10
Resources						
Judicial	_[a]	_[a]	.88	_[a]	_[a]	−.12
Nonjudicial	_[a]	_[a]	.95	_[a]	_[a]	−.10

[a]Not available.

(r = .88) and nonjudicial (r = .95) resources parallels the respective correlations between judicial and nonjudicial staff, that is, the effect of nonjudicial variables is slightly stronger. As previous findings have suggested, nonjudicial clerks may be as important as judges for the smooth functioning of this court. But, as we saw in chapter 5, the reorganization of this court into a bureaucratic agency that relies primarily upon civil-servant personnel is a fundamental challenge to the traditions and entrenched positions of members of the legal community.

At all three points in time, none of the measures of the personnel and resources is associated with payment effectiveness. These findings suggest that whatever claims were paid back to creditors had little, if anything, to do with the formal input from the personnel of this court.

The other side of the effectiveness coin is an interorganizational dimension. In the case of the bankruptcy court this dimension involves the lawyers and trustees whose work revolves around the court but who are not directly employed by it. That is, it is also necessary to discover whether lawyers and trustees benefit in terms of income for labor. Does this variable account for the number of cases terminated? More specifically, is the structure of the bankruptcy court more beneficial for its organizational matrix than it is for its clients, be they debtors or creditors? The analysis of this pivotal issue is critical for understanding the present dilemma of the bankruptcy court. Let us turn, then, to an analysis of the relative effect of these factors on the number of bankruptcy cases terminated.

Table 6-3 shows the separate, direct, and joint effects of bankruptcy filings, the organizational matrix, and full-time judges on the terminations of the bankruptcy court in 1950, 1960, and 1970.[4]

Table 6-3
Zero-Order Correlations (r), Standardized Regression Coefficients (b^*), and Multiple Correlation Coefficients (R^2) for the Tasks, Organizational Matrix, and Personnel on the Effectiveness of the Bankruptcy Court in 1950, 1960, and 1970

		Terminations		
		'50	'60	'70
Filings	r	.77	.52	.99
	b^*	.78	.94	.97
Organizational matrix	r	.14	.21	.79
	b^*	.08	−.41	.06
Full-time judges	r	.12	.14	.87
	b^*	.12	−.16	−.03
	R^2	.62	.38	.99

At all three points in time, the zero-order correlation between filings and terminations is moderately strong (1950, $r = .77$; 1960, $r = .52$; 1970, $r = .99$). This is not surprising since terminations are, in one respect, the other side of filings. However, the drop in the simple correlation between these variables in 1960 raises a question that will be returned to shortly.

Like the changing effect of full-time judges from 1950 to 1970, the organizational matrix reveals a consistently stronger set of correlations with terminations in 1950 ($r = .14$), 1960 ($r = .21$), and 1970 ($r = .79$); moreover, the dramatic change occurred from 1960 to 1970. The findings of chapter 4 reveal that by 1960 the environmental profile of a district explained the earnings of lawyers and trustees (see table 4-3); the findings of chapter 5 were that since 1950 the presence of lawyers and trustees has been a significant factor in explaining the number of full-time judges (see table 5-5). While this matrix of professionals did not affect the disposition of bankruptcy cases until 1970, that impact is now unmistakable: the organizational matrix, the community of bankruptcy specialists, now affects all aspects of the bankruptcy court.

The combined effect (R^2) of filings, organizational matrix, and full-time judges increased from 1950 ($R^2 = .62$) to 1970 ($R^2 = .99$), but with a noticeable drop in 1960 ($R^2 = .38$). Why? Though the court was disposing of more cases (see table 6-1) without the aid of full-time judges, in the final analysis this situation appears to have affected the work process of this court, for the combination of these factors simply accounted for less of the variance in terminations. This is also reflected in the lower correlation between filings and terminations discussed earlier. But by 1970, these findings suggest, the calculus in the termination of cases was a carefully modulated balance of task-oriented, professional, and judicial inputs.

The organizational matrix—the lawyers and trustees—of the bankruptcy court have had a rather secure position in the court. By 1970, this "ring" may have included judges as well. The growing number of bankruptcy cases in the period under study provided increasing work for lawyers, trustees, and judges. Thus, the court has become a forum in which lawyers, trustees, and judges have worked together to meet their own professional needs.[5]

Effectiveness is a political variable. These findings summarize an important paradox suggested in the beginning of this book. The significantly increased influence of nonjudicial personnel and resources in the twenty years under study suggests that the court can maintain its adjudicatory appearance due to the increased clerical support that precedes the actual courtroom decision. That is, the relative effectiveness of adjudication must rely upon external, nonjudicial supports to prepare, if not decide, the cases that come before the judge (see table 6-2). However, the fact that these nonjudicial supports may be capable of making a final decision, rather than only preparing a decision, is an organizational possibility that challenges the political network of bankruptcy court.

Effectiveness: Who Benefits?

Effectiveness is neither a neutral nor an apolitical aspect of organizational development. The bankruptcy court adjudicates the legal disputes that arise between debtors and creditors. As the court presently exists, creditors find the organization to their advantage; moreover, the organization of the court works to the benefit of "wealthier" debtors, or those debtors who tend to bring business-type cases to the court.

The final question for analysis is uncovered, then, by scrutinizing the debates over effectiveness. Those groups who introduce the question of effectiveness include judges, creditors, practicing attorneys, consumer groups, legal scholars, and the Administrative Office of the Courts. Court effectiveness raises two questions when considered in the context of transformation: what has caused the present structure of the court to be ineffective, and what will be the role of an effective court for debtors in the future?

The Causes of the Court's Ineffectiveness

Creditors, Lawyers, and Judges. Presentation of court testimony assumes that some type of reform is necessary. That is, those groups who specify the cause of the present ineffectiveness of the court agree that the court must be changed; however, strong differences are expressed as to how that should be done. The court's ineffectiveness is attributed to different causes in the testimony of various groups. In the words of a spokesperson for creditors, "The spread of home mortgage financing and consumer credit to the majority of the population has increased the potential for consumer bankruptcies and strained the administration of bankruptcy laws, but it has not changed the philosophy determining when such relief should be available (*Senate Hearings* 1975, p. 139).

From the perspective of creditors, lawyers, and judges, the availability of money is the cause of the ineffectiveness of the present court (see *House Hearings* 1976, p. 1266). These creditors, judges, and lawyers, who have been a part of the court's development, argue that ineffectiveness is a result of a growing open-credit economy. None of these groups makes reference to the changing occupational structure of the post-World War II period. However, this variable has been a primary factor in the increased number of bankruptcies. The political position expressed by creditors, and shared by judges and lawyers, shows little awareness of the actual causes of increased consumer bankruptcy. (See *Senate Hearings* 1975, pp. 185-215; also see *House Hearings* 1975, pp. 897-908.)

Consumer Groups. Ineffectiveness is not perceived the same way by all groups. Consumer advocates, who have had no part in the court's development, see ineffectiveness as a result of the very structure of the organization, which has emphasized business interests rather than consumer interests (also see *House Hearings* 1976, pp. 1699-1717). In the words of a spokesperson for the Consumer Law Center, "The present law is inadequate for consumers because of its inability to respond to the needs of the non-business debtor . . . . Decisions in bankruptcy are dominated by business considerations and the interests of the business enterprise which are creditors in the process" (*Senate Hearings* 1975, p. 306). Our findings support the conclusions of this consumer law advocate. The court is increasingly oriented to the needs of business (*House Hearings* 1976, pp. 1700-1701). These two groups reach distinctly different conclusions.

The consumer law advocates are outsiders to the history of this court; thus, they have no vested interest in maintaining its present structure. In addition, they come to the debates on court reform as the most direct representatives of the court's invisible client, the consumer debtor. Therefore, they are compelled to present the most accurate and challenging assessment of the court.

The Future Role of the Bankruptcy Court

What will be the impact of increased bankruptcies on the economy? Is it a serious economic issue? Why is it important to create an effective court for the future? In assessing this aspect of the problem, consideration will first be given to legal experts.

Legal Scholars. One of them has stated, "What is the impact of the rising bankruptcy rates on the economy? My own opinion is that it is not significant. Remember that 90% of the bankruptcy cases are consumer bankruptcies and that most of the extenders of consumer credit . . . operate with more emphasis on volume than on careful investigation of credit worthiness" (*House Hearings* 1975, p. 341). According to this legal scholar,[6] the court's ultimate effect upon the economy will be rather minor regardless of the increased number of bankruptcies. Insofar as "experts" comment on the importance of transforming the organizational structure of this court, they ultimately suggest that the outcome is of little consequence.

Judges. Judges in bankruptcy argue that "there is scant realization of the magnitude of the remaining 10 percent of business filings, or the number and variety of legal controversies that arise in such a single major case" (*House Hearings* 1975, p. 511). That is, judges in bankruptcy argue that the complexity of business bankruptcy cases demands an adjudicatory forum. As the court has developed since 1950, business-type cases have become a critical issue for this court. Business bankrupts do not have a direct advocate during the processes of reform;

however, the judges' position concerning the future of the court emphasizes the centrality of business interests in the development of this organization.

Thus, while legal scholars state that the implications of bankruptcy cases are relatively unimportant and rest their argument with consumer cases, judges state that bankruptcy cases are complex and rest their argument with business cases. The dialogue among political actors concerning the court's future effectiveness reveals antithetical positions.

Several groups suggest how and for whom the court should be effective in the future.

Consumer Groups. Consumer law advocates call for the introduction of effective educational devices within the organization of the court or agency in order to make it effective for consumers in the future. Not only should the bankruptcy process handle consumer cases, but it should also service the needs of such individuals by providing more long-term guidance (*House Hearings* 1976, pp. 1337-41). Only in this way can the bankruptcy process provide a meaningful "fresh start." Implicit in this argument is the concept of reform through educational services, a significant theme in many contemporary social-change debates.[7]

Practicing Attorneys. One "entrepreneurial" lawyer who has been a part of this court's formation through its organizational matrix promotes another device for the court's future effectiveness: the introduction of computers to process consumer reorganization cases. A lawyer's task in a court of law is limited to serving as a representative for a client in the court. Lawyers are formally employed by the client. The analysis of the court's development showed that by 1960 the organizational matrix was an integral factor in this organization. This lawyer's support for the introduction of computers as a necessary device for an effective court suggests that lawyers' services have extended beyond legal representation. Their work in the area of bankruptcy law has given them the opportunity to develop a "business" in bankruptcy:

The computer services with which I am associated serves Chapter XIII trustees in many parts of the United States. During fiscal year 1975 our customers filed final reports in more than 4000 successfully completed cases. The average attorney fee paid to debtor's attorney was $225.48. The cases remained active for an average of 38.5 months. Thus, the debtors had an attorney on call for 38.5 months at an average cost of $5.86 per month. The debtor's total cost including attorney fees, court costs, trustees' fees and trustees' expenses, plus interest which was paid to creditors through the plan amounted to a cost of less than 16¢ out of each dollar (actually it was 15.8¢). This is the equivalent of an annual percentage rate on a consumer load of 10.75% on simple interest. (*Senate Hearings* 1975, p. 580)

This lawyer argues that through the introduction of this technology, the court can guarantee a more effective legal procedure for the consumer and simultaneously maintain both the trustee and lawyer as important personnel in the adjudication of cases. Moreover, this "entrepreneur" has other supporters, like the one who stated, "Granting that such a system [data processing] is appropriate and computers should be utilized, is it unreasonable to ask why it cannot be done within the present system?" (*Senate Hearings* 1975, 399).

But perhaps the most direct threat to this stratum of the legal profession is the issue of debtor counseling. Hence, these attorneys' opposition to this proposal is presented in clear and strong language: "No one denies that social counseling is advisable. But such counseling is entirely sensible today through recourse to community resources or through the auspices of a counselor appended to the court staff much as the probation office functions in relation to the U.S. district court" (*Senate Hearings* 1975, p. 400; also see *House Hearings* 1976, pp. 1264-65). The myth of availability, anytime, day or night, is an important aspect in the perpetuation of professional dominance and control (see Freidson 1972). It becomes imperative, then, that professionals constantly reconstruct and advocate this ideology; but this is especially critical during moments when the professional's control and autonomy is in possible jeopardy.

Legal Scholars. Legal scholars present yet another avenue for consideration regarding the future effectiveness of the bankruptcy court—improvement of the discharge provision of bankruptcy law. The discharge provision guarantees bankrupts that their property will be protected through the bankruptcy process, that not all of their possessions and earnings will be confiscated:

The discharge provisions of the Bankruptcy Act are frequently referred to as the embodiment of the "fresh start" policy. Congress has steadily strengthened and implemented this policy in each successive Bankruptcy Act and in an amendment to the Act of 1898. The Supreme Court has likewise given increasingly sympathetic construction to the discharge provisions.
   [Critical legal decisions have attempted to work on] the premise . . . that it is better for society generally for a debtor to be free of the burden of past indebtedness so that he will be motivated to exert his best efforts to provide for the future needs of his family and himself than for him to struggle for economic survival while paying or fending off creditors holding old debts. (*House Hearings* 1975, p. 159)

Thus, legal scholars approach the improved effectiveness of the court as a legal question. The Congress has the power to make the court a more viable organization for consumers by better insuring a meaningful fresh start.

Interestingly, one legal scholar raises the problems of counselling debtors from yet another perspective: "What I fear for is that this is what we have been doing in a way with the welfare program and with many other programs. The Congress will, in effect, although perhaps not by intent, legislate the morality of another group. That group is this near-poor group that ends up in bankruptcy (*House Hearings* 1976, p. 866). Again, it is this "outsider" in the history of this organization who presents the more subtle, though critical, implications of court reform.

Conclusion: Reform for Whom?

Consumer advocates' recommendations rest upon education, lawyers' recommendations rest upon improved technology, and legal scholars' recommendations rest upon improved laws. There is little overlap in these suggestions. Although the different groups agree that some form of organizational change or reform is necessary, it is clear that they point to different causes of the court's ineffectiveness, see different degrees of urgency, and have called for different actions to create a more effective court. A lack of agreement seems to be the basic issue. Administrative reform is a significant theme in American history. Couched in an ideology that has sought to bring the processes of government "closer" to the people, such efforts have often yielded very different results.

Reform of the bankruptcy court poses a number of possibilities to "solve" the problems of the present organization of the court. The configuration of each reform proposal presents new organizational outcomes—new strategies for organizing bankruptcy law. One outcome may be the establishment of an administrative structure to process, rather than adjudicate, bankruptcy cases. A second outcome may be the establishment of an autonomous bankruptcy court resulting from an attempt to give greater prestige to bankruptcy law. And a third outcome may be that the organization of the court will not change. Plans may be introduced to reorganize the court, but such changes may not be implemented.

The task demands of this court were the product of changes in the environmental profile of a district. From 1950 to 1970 changes within the monopoly sector, the competitive sector, and the white-collar sector of the U.S. Federal District have specified a more variable and complex task structure. In the process of reform, the variability and complexity of the task structure has been epitomized by two opposing political groups, representing consumer and business interests. That is, the variability and complexity of the bankruptcy court's task is not merely an organizational issue: it is also a political problem.

The organizational matrix of the bankruptcy court is also the product of changes in the environment of the bankruptcy court. By 1960 the important environmental variables of the court specified the organizational matrix. Moreover, the organizational matrix was a critical variable for explaining the court's intraorganizational response to these changing environmental pressures. When the court faces possible reform, the organizational matrix will be, therefore, a well-organized and cohesive group with a strong political and economic interest in the organizational outcome of reform.

Since 1950 the development of the court has generated unstated conflicts. The realities of court reform transform these unstated conflicts into overt ones. For example, until the debate over court reform, the importance of the organizational matrix as a controlling group in the court was not stated. Until the debate over court reform, the importance of "wealthier" bankruptcy cases for the functioning of the court was not stated. "Solutions" to these conflicts that become apparent at the moment of reform cannot be complete: reformers must address themselves to the needs of lawyers as well as to the need for creating a source of revenue to pay for the operation of the court. Since court reform does not appear *de novo,* the strategies for change that may be implemented must be worked out within the parameters established throughout the court's history. Court reform—organizational transformation—is a "more or less incomplete" set of organizational possibilities designed to meet the immediate demands and opposing pressures of this organization.

Notes

1. This is, of course, most clearly stated in "Politics as a Vocation" (1946c).

2. As Marcuse (1971) points out, this leads to one of the most problematic aspects of the Weberian schema because the statements concerning parliamentary skills assume the viability of charismatic leadership.

3. Claims are generally divided into three categories: "priority," "secured," and "unsecured." Priority claims are those obligations which, while unsecured, are nevertheless accorded a specific priority in payment as prescribed in Section 64 of the Bankruptcy Act. Priority claims must be paid in full from the general estate before unsecured general claims can be paid. Secured claims are those of creditors whose claims are secured by a security interest (either consensual or statutory) in assets of the estate. Such claims are not paid from the general estate but rather may be paid from the proceeds of the sale of the specific property in which security interest is held. Unsecured claims are those claims that are entitled to neither a priority status nor secured status. These claims are entitled to participate in the general estate remaining from the liquidation after provable priority claims and costs of administration are paid.

4. The beta coefficients shown for 1960 and 1970 must be interpreted with caution due to the high intercorrelation between the independent variables (see appendix D) and the attendant problems of multicollinearity. However,

the zero-order correlations and the explained variance reveal important findings for final consideration in this phase of the study.

5. The melding of legal "roles" of lawyers and judges is also revealed in the pretrial conference. Since 1940, pretrial conferences have accounted for over 40 percent of the dispositions of civil matters in the federal district courts (see Heydebrand and Seron, forthcoming). The pretrial conference was formally adopted by the Judicial Conference in 1938, one year after the "court-packing" fight in which Roosevelt rested his case on the need for greater efficiency and rationality within the judiciary (Schubert 1960).

In a pretrial conference, the judge may call a meeting of lawyers without the presence of clients. The purpose of this meeting is to clarify the issues and the scope of the controversy in question, and generally to articulate the legal parameters under consideration. This is a significant departure from a traditional adversarial procedure in that the judge, rather than the lawyers, initiates the final settlement (Rosenberg 1964). Like plea bargaining in criminal matters (Blumberg 1970), pretrial conferences reflect a general trend toward a more relaxed adversarial model of litigation (Glaser 1968).

6. "Starting in October, 1974, there has been an increase in business bankruptcies that is unparalleled in this history of the country. In the first nine months of fiscal year 1975, a total of 184,655 cases of all types has been filed under the act, which represents a 35.2 percent increase over filings in fiscal year 1975" (*House Hearings* 1975, p. 4).

7. Lemert's (1970, p. 34) analysis of juvenile court reform in California reveals that early legislation on child welfare grew out of a "puritan" concern with education for developing self-discipline and became the guideline for California reform schools. Also see Bowles and Gintis (1976).

7

Conclusion

How are courts reformed? What organizational factors create an environment open to the possibility of reform? For whom is reform an effective process of social change? These have been the organizing questions of this book.

A number of facts have been dramatically revealed. Perhaps the most salient one is that the lawyers and judges of this court, both in the process of formation and transformation, often disregard the interests of individuals, in this case the interests of bankrupts. This takes place in various ways. In its present structure, the court is more responsive to the legal profession than it is to debtors and, during debates on court reform, practicing attorneys and judges dominate the debates of this political arena.

The class relations of the court come to the fore during the debates on reform. In considering the place of the legal profession in the development of the bankruptcy court, it was suggested that its members are part of a "new middle class," since they owe their very existence to the fact that they contribute to the process of capital accumulation. Both corporate and consumer bankruptcies are the product of the changing dynamics of the political economy. So long as the economy can provide mechanisms for the accumulation of capital in spite of bankruptcies, the members of the new middle class are a necessary part of the court's formation. In part, the increased participation of lawyers and trustees must be understood as a necessary by-product of capitalist development. A division of labor is not a self-generated phenomenon. In the case before us, the division of labor among lawyers, trustees, and judges will persist as long as there is a process of economic accumulation that supports them.

There is no neutral, apolitical direction in which processes of change inevitably move. More "rational" procedures may be introduced to improve the efficiency of the bankruptcy court. In large part, the possibility of introducing these techniques seem to be dependent upon their potential service to specific groups—lawyers, judges, and creditors.

The boundaries placed upon the court during its development limit the possibilities of reform; hence, the proposed "solutions" will in fact benefit the legal profession, not the public interest. It will benefit those who have been day-to-day participants in the history of this court.

The significance of introducing computerization cannot be ignored. The apparently innocuous cry for computerization, in the name of rationality and efficiency, actually has important political implications, for computerization provides the legal profession with a legitimate mechanism to demand continued

125

control. Given the severe task demands on this as well as on other courts, the legal profession actually has no alternative but to support various technological strategies for the coordination and disposition of court cases. However, like the position of doctors in medicine, their dominance appears to be solid so long as the profession controls the technology (Alford 1975; Freidson 1972). After all, in both fields only a portion of professional labor can possibly be mechanized, or so the proponents of this argument assert. Yet, if it is possible to computerize the work associated with part of a relatively straightforward legal procedure such as consumer bankruptcy, is it not possible eventually to computerize the entire process? Seen in this light, computerization, introduced as the panacea by the more traditional interest groups of court reform, is in fact a historically specific, a "more or less incomplete" solution in the face of ever pressing social demands on our legal institutions.

But computerization is, at present, only one aspect of this debate. During the 1977 Congress a "compromise" bill was presented. Two features describe this bill (H.R. 6) and the essence of the conflict that was documented in chapters 3 to 6. First, this reform proposes the establishment of a separate, autonomous court with the appointment of judges by the president for lifetime tenure. Clearly, this proposal bows to the demands articulated by the bankruptcy legal profession for it was repeatedly argued that the improved status of the court will positively serve the public interest. Perhaps ironically, though, this bill proposes an even more "prestigious," i.e., autonomous, court than the judges had themselves bargained for. Whereas the Judges' Bill proposed that judges be appointed for fifteen years under Article I, this bill proposes that they be appointed for life under Article III.

The second facet of this bill is the proposed Office of Trustees in the Department of Justice. By contrast to the first reform measure, this proposal bows to the more bureaucratic bent of the Commission's Bill. That is, this agency answers social reformers' plea for more equitable treatment of consumer bankrupts. However, affected consumers would still require the counsel of an attorney since all cases will, under this proposal, be heard by a judge.

The voice of one rather obviously concerned group has been silent up to this point in the debate. The Judicial Conference of the United States—the formal organ of federal court judges—did not send representatives to testify. However, the proposed compromise bill has quickly altered this situation. In response to this bill, judges

RESOLVED that the Judicial Conference of the United States opposes legislation pending in the Congress which would convert bankruptcy courts into Article I or Article III courts, and giving Article III tenure to referees in bankruptcy.

The Chief Justice is authorized to designate an ad hoc committee to draft a supporting memorandum in implementation of this resolution.

The Conference especially requests that at an appropriate time it be given an opportunity to present its views on this subject matter to the Congress. (1977)

In 1970 Burger, in one of his many speeches on judicial administration, specifically argued for the more efficient processing of bankruptcy cases. The problems of courts cannot, he has contended, be solved by simply adding judicial positions; more importantly, new methods, machinery, management, and trained administrative personnel must be introduced into our court system. "In the supermarket age we are trying to operate the courts with cracker-barrel corner grocer methods and equipment—vintage 1900" (1970, p. iv). In essence, Burger has consistently argued that the courts must introduce techniques that will bring these organizations into the twentieth century. The answer to the crisis of the courts is better, more rational administration.

Clearly then, this compromise bill contradicts present developments in the courts and must, from this perspective, be seen as a "regressive" policy shift. Echoing the modern ideology of administrative due process, Burger has assumed that more rational rules, procedures, administrative techniques, and management can be separated from the quality of justice; in fact it is his position, and the position of other reformers, that such solutions improve the quality of justice. But this distinction is part of the ideological baggage of a liberal tradition. Most organizational innovations, including bureaucratic reforms, may further camouflage, but do not mitigate, the fundamentally unequal social and economic relations of American society.

This all suggests a rather pessimistic conclusion. Reform is not a process that inevitably achieves better service to its public. Does this mean that one should disengage oneself from efforts at reform?

The analysis of the formation and transformation of the bankruptcy court has revealed that the organization of the court creates a focal point for legitimating relations among social strata. Since its formation in 1938, the court has provided a mechanism whereby groups of lawyers and judges—"rings and cliques"—have been able to serve their own interests as a group, but in the name of providing a forum for the adjudication of bankruptcy cases. Thus, as they confront the debates on court reform they do so as a relatively strong and unified group.

By contrast, legal scholars, consumer law advocates, and representatives of labor who seek to change the organizational structure of the court do so in a rather naive and limited way. For example, they often speak to narrow aspects of reform without consideration for the implications of their position. Or, they oppose the reform without providing an alternative in its place. Neither tactic is adequate, particularly when the opposition has a well-formulated plan that does address the total picture, in this case the organization of the court.

Two issues are apparent. First, in order to challenge meaningfully the established structure of organizations that do not equitably serve their public, it is necessary for reformers to enter the public arena long before change is actually at issue. It will be necessary to engage in the formation, as well as the transformation, of an organization. Secondly, alternatives must be formulated that address the total issue at the same time that the weaknesses of the opposition's position is brought forward. For example, if laws are to be written to serve clearly the interest of consumers, then it is necessary to engage in the formulation of those laws. Without a commitment to both of these issues, reforms will continue to be, as the analysis of Congressional testimony suggests, a conservative response to a libertarian impetus.

At the same time, the limitations of reform within the context of American society must be emphasized. One must be willing to engage in reform, but with a recognition of its limitations. For it is only with an awareness of those limitations that reform may provide a vehicle for some degree of significant and meaningful social change.

There is a growing body of literature in both sociology and history that has documented the introduction of reforms in American society. The common theme in this literature is that the myriads of reform agencies that have proliferated since the Progressive Era ultimately serve to maintain a status quo. Though they are couched in an ideology of social change and equal opportunity, their ultimate result has perpetuated a structured inequality.

Kolko's (1967, 1976) work on the Progressive Era documents that control of politics by business, rather than the political regulation of the economy, was a significant phenomenon in this period. For example, by 1906 business favored the introduction of the Federal Trade Commission, an agency established in the name of regulating monopolization but which became a vehicle to legitimate monopolization. Kolko concludes that control through government regulation may become a means of maintaining economic order and political security for business. A crucial factor in the American experience was, and is, the nature of economic power that demanded political tools as a way to rationalize and control the economy.

Weinstein (1968) has demonstrated that the move toward city management was supported by small businessmen represented by the local chamber of commerce, again a phenomenon of the turn of the century. "The centralization of power, or the removal of decision-making from 'politics,' favored businessmen over working men or white-collar employees. In no area of political or social reform did small businessmen more clearly demonstrate the force of this logic than in the movements for city commissions and manager movements" (pp. 92–93). Insofar as the business corporation provided a model of efficiency, its structure and rationale were duplicated in city governments. Between 1910 and 1919, the Socialist Party led a campaign opposing these forms of government because they eliminated the ward system, restricted ethnic representation, centralized control, restricted room for opposition, eliminated political parties, and made elections into personality contests.

The historical examples of these two reforms during the Progressive Era find analogies in more contemporary settings. O'Connor's thesis of the growing "social-industrial complex" asserts that the marriage between the state and the monopoly sector will be a necessary by-product of advanced capitalist society. The theme that draws this history together is that increasing numbers of social welfare agencies of various kinds more often than not serve the welfare of business, rather than the welfare of workers.

The question then arises: do rational bureaucratic agencies provide the panacea for social change that their proponents support? Organizationally these agencies share characteristics that mirror the structure of corporate organizations. McConnell (1966) has argued that the ground rules articulated by Taylor for worker management became the ideal of government reform. This was particularly so in the establishment of the forestry service during Theodore Roosevelt's presidency. Scientific management, as articulated by Taylor, sought to separate the work process into discrete categories of work:

The preconception of the process before it is set in motion, the visualization of each worker's activities before they have actually begun, the definition of each function along with the manner of its performance and the time it will consume, the control and checking of the ongoing process once it is under way, and the assessment of results upon completion of each stage of the process—all of these aspects of production have been removed from the shop floor to the management's office. (Braverman 1974, pp. 124–125)

That Taylor's work has laid the groundwork for much contemporary organizational research is an interesting facet of modern sociology (Perrow 1972).

The formulation of scientific management complements Weber's assumptions concerning the rationalization of bureaucratic organization.[1] Weber makes his case for the claimed superiority of rational bureaucratic control on purely technical grounds. Above all else, Weber concludes, official rules, hierarchy, and so on, are technically more effective and therefore will be inevitable. But what Weber fails to consider is for whom these tend to be more effective. That is, he assumes that rational bureaucratization is an apolitical process, though this is not to say that he assumes it to be without negative repercussions.

The analysis of the bankruptcy court, as well as the examples of reform cited earlier, demonstrate that reform is, in fact, generally more effective for some than for others. The reliance upon scientific management, business techniques, human relations models, or more recently computerization in the initiation of agencies of reform has been shown to be a vehicle for the continued control by business over labor. Moreover, business must support these strategies of reform in order to maintain a hegemonic position.

Thus, reform in the twentieth century has often been supported by business as a tool to maintain control over labor. These reform agencies organizationally parallel business organizations and use various techniques of scientific management as a guide for their establishment. The organizational structure of these agencies of reform tends to complement the aims of its reformers.

Returning to the case of the bankruptcy court, some important clarifications emerge. The push toward codification, or rationalization, of the law is not supported by practicing lawyers and judges. In fact, just the contrary is the case. Those who have been external to the court's formation—the members of the Commission, representatives of labor, consumer law advocates, and legal scholars—support a codification of the law into rules that guide bankruptcy procedure.

The interest groups concerned with the bankruptcy court form a political continuum from liberal to conservative. The more conservative group (in this context it is fair to refer to the judges, lawyers, and creditors as more conservative) seeks to maintain the substantive foundation of a traditional court. The more liberal faction (consumer law advocates, representatives of labor, and legal scholars) supports the codification, or rationalization, of the law. However, this more liberal faction is not conscious of the political limitations of their positions, the ways in which it implicitly complements and supports the dominant structure of reform strategies in American society. It is the judges themselves who make reference to this point. They are acutely aware of the fact that the reform of bankruptcy court as suggested by the Commission's Bill, further removes the court from the people. However, this is not to conclude that the more liberal groups are in fact the conservatives and vice-versa. Rather, it is to point out that those who are most directly under attack in the process of reform may be the first ones to understand fully the implications of that process, though perhaps for the "wrong" reasons. The judges' solution, or reform, is a self-interested one, a reform that seeks to upgrade the status of this specialized area of the law.

So, as reform of the bankruptcy court presently stands, neither the Judges' Bill, the Commission's Bill, or the compromise bill can fundamentally maintain and safeguard the rights of the consumer bankrupt.

The legal order balances three potentially contradictory elements: formal legal rationality, or equality before the law; the need to maintain order, or control the public interest; and the need to maintain the organizational structure of a court, or its adjudicatory appearance (Balbus 1973). As long as marginal groups do not consciously challenge these parameters of the legal order, the dominant structure will be maintained intact. The more liberal groups of bankruptcy court reform are not conscious of the limitations of their position, the subtle yet distinct ways in which support for a more codified, formal law ultimately maintains rather than changes the structure of American society.

Then how might the bankruptcy court be reformed? When groups participate in processes of reform it must be seen for what it is. Reform is not, and cannot be, a fundamental restructuring of the processes and relations of society. Careful analysis must be given to the pros and cons of removing a forum that adjudicates cases and replacing it with a forum that administers cases. The dynamics of this decision are further complicated by the fact that more conservative judges commonly profess to support the maintenance of the organization of the court whereas more liberal groups seek to alter that forum. Thus, consideration must be given to whether it is possible to change a sector of the legal structure, the court house, without also addressing the environment surrounding the court. That is, a more fundamental liberal challenge must also address directions for changing the way in which lawyers are made available to their publics. If this process is inequitable, is the only solution to remove their availability for some and maintain it for others? After all, the ultimate implication of the Commission's Bill and bureaucracies in general is that lawyers will not be used by consumers. But this is not to say that businesses and corporations will not use lawyers.

Within the dominant legal structure, is it possible to maintain an adjudicatory forum that simultaneously provides more equitable and more meaningful legal counsel? This question articulates the challenge that reformers of our legal system must address.

Note

1. For a more elaborate discussion of this point, using the work of March and Simon as an example, see Heydebrand (1973a).

Appendix A: Preparation of Data of the Bankruptcy Court

The data used to examine the bankruptcy court in 1950, 1960, and 1970 were collected from three sources: the Bureau of the Census, the National Conference Board, and the Bankruptcy Division of the Administrative Office of the United States Courts.

Bureau of the Census Data

Data collected by the census were used as measures of the court's environment. Computer tapes made available by the census were recoded and aggregated to conform to the specifications of this study. The U.S. Federal District is composed of counties; the counties that describe a district were ascertained from the *United States Code Annotated, Title 28* (1969). Using programs available from the *Statistical Package for the Social Sciences* (Nie 1975), it was then possible to recode the census bureau's county identification number and aggregate counties into units conforming to the U.S. Federal District; thus, these units reflect the actual characteristics of the court's immediate environment.

From 1950 to 1970 the number of districts changed. To make the units comparable from 1950 to 1970 those districts that had changed were combined or dropped. Therefore, the analyses presented in chapters 3, 4, 5, and 6 are based upon eighty-four units (see table A-1). This study also excludes the territorial courts of local jurisdiction, i.e., Canal Zone, Guam, Puerto Rico, and Virgin Islands.

I am grateful to Howard Zager for writing a special program to correct the 1950 *City and County Data Book* tape (U.S. Bureau of the Census), and to Andrew Rollings for help in the preparation of these data.

National Conference Board

The National Conference Board collects data on mergers each month by city. The twelve monthly reports, i.e., *Announcements of Mergers and Acquisitions*, for 1960 and 1970 were used to collect these data. The mergers were collapsed by city of purchasing company and then the number of mergers by city was combined within the U.S. Federal District. The median assets of purchasing companies were ascertained in a similar way. These data were punched on cards suitable for input; they were then added to the data files for the respective year.

Table A-1
District Changes and Additions from 1950 to 1970

1950	1960	1970
––	Hawaii	Hawaii (dropped)
California North	California North	California North California East (combined)
California South	California South	California South California Central (combined)
Florida South	Florida South	Florida South Florida Middle (combined)
––	Hawaii	Hawaii (dropped)
Louisiana East	Louisiana East	Louisiana East Louisiana Middle (combined)
South Carolina East South Carolina West	South Carolina East South Carolina West	South Carolina (combined)

Bankruptcy Division of the Administrative Office of the
United States Courts

All statistics on the bankruptcy court were collected by the Bankruptcy Division of the Administrative Office of the United States Courts; reports are published annually by the government.[1] The definition of each variable that was used in this study is comparable by decade. Data collection by the Bankruptcy Division is part of their task as defined by legislative mandate in order to keep a record of the court's development. As was the case with the census data, the data on some districts were combined to make them comparable in 1950, 1960, and 1970 (see table A-1).

I am grateful to Berkely Wright and Thomas Beitleman of the Bankruptcy Division for clarifying the precise definition of these records. I would also like to thank Natasha Krinitzky for preparing these data for computer readable form.

Data were analyzed on the IBM 370 Computer at New York University and Yale University. I would like to thank Bert Holland of the Computer Center at New York University for his unusual patience in helping me "de-bug" many programs.

Note

1. See the *Tables on Bankruptcy Statistics with Reference to Bankruptcy Cases Commenced and Terminated in the United States District Courts During*

The Fiscal Year Ending June 30, 1950 (1950); *Tables on Bankruptcy Statistics with Reference to Bankruptcy Cases Commenced and Terminated in the United States District Courts During the Fiscal Year Ending June 30, 1960* (1960); *Tables on Bankruptcy Statistics with Reference to Bankruptcy Cases Commenced and Terminated in the United States District Courts During the Fiscal Year Ending June 30, 1969* (1969). The Administrative Office did not collect detailed data on this court from 1970 to 1974; therefore, it was necessary to substitute 1969 data.

Appendix B: Steps in the
Analysis of Court Reform

Analysis of the debates on court reform included ascertaining the interest groups of court reform, the organizational issues of court reform, and the positions of groups on each of these issues of court reform.

The interest groups of court reform were ascertained through informant interviews with Tom Burgum, the Deputy Counsel of the Senate Subcommittee of Improvements in Judicial Machinery; Alan Parker, the Chief Counsel for the House Subcommittee on Civil and Constitutional Rights; Philip Shuchman, Professor at the School of Law of the University of Connecticut (a member of the Commission to study the bankruptcy court); and Charles Seligson (deceased), Professor at the School of Law of New York University (the chairperson of the Commission to study the bankruptcy court). Each interviewee listed basically the same groups: judges in bankruptcy, practicing attorneys, creditors, consumer law advocates, legal scholars, representatives of organized labor, the representative of the Bankruptcy Division of the Administrative Office of the United States Courts, and representatives of the United States Attorney's Office. The detailed review of the Congressional testimony (to be described below) also confirmed that these groups represented organizations that participated in the debates on court reform.

However, these groups were not "equally" represented. . Table B-1 shows the number of testimonies for each interest group. Clearly, these debates are

Table B-1
Number of Testimonies by Interest Group[a]

	House hearings	Senate hearings
Judges	15	6
Practicing attorneys	31	10
Creditors/bankers	22	20
Consumer law advocates	3	3
Legal scholars	16	10
Labor	4	5
Administrative office	3	1
U.S. Attorney	3	3
	$n = 97$	$n = 58$

[a]The sum shown represents the total number of times all individuals testified. That is, one person may have testified two or three times before both the House and Senate Committees. Each formal presentation is counted separately.

structurally skewed in favor of certain groups. As one legal scholar testified, "If you look over the list of witnesses before the committees on their versions of these bills, it becomes evident that one, perhaps at best two of the witnesses can be said fairly to speak for the small personal consumer bankrupt" (*House Hearings* 1976, p. 871).

A number of representatives from executive agencies (i.e., SEC, FTC, ICC) were also present at these hearings. Most of these "groups" testified on specific aspects of bankruptcy law (to be described below). The position of these groups has been indicated in footnotes at the appropriate place. Since these representatives were concerned only with very narrow aspects of reform, they were omitted from this analysis.

One other point is apparent from table B-1: most representatives that testified before these committees are part of the legal profession, but often from very different areas of that profession. This factor made the group of "practicing attorneys" particularly difficult to categorize. To avoid overlapping categories, this group included only those who spoke as attorneys primarily involved with bankruptcy litigation. Therefore, attorneys who taught law and occasionally represented clients were counted as legal scholars, not practicing attorneys.

In developing the research proposal in the fall of 1973, a careful review of the *Report of the Commission on Bankruptcy Law* (1973) revealed that a major suggestion for reform centered around structural changes in the organization of the court. This finding was confirmed by informant interviews with all bankruptcy judges in the Eastern and Southern Districts of New York during the summer of 1973. The Commission's proposal of an administrative agency to handle bankruptcy cases was a major suggestion of the *Report*. From an organizational perspective this suggestion is a fundamental challenge to the collegial structure of this court as it presently exists.

The Commission's Bill and the Judges' Bill[1] were then carefully reviewed to determine the congruence between the organizational perspective developed for analyzing court reform and the actual suggestions that these bills contain. The review of each bill confirmed the possibility of examining court reform from the perspective outlined in chapter 2.

This study focuses on one aspect of reform, that is, the debate over *organizational innovations*. However, there are many other topics attached to this proposal, for example, public or municipal bankruptcies (*House Hearings* 1976, pp. 633–755; *Senate Hearings* 1975, pp. 684–719), stockbrokerage bankruptcies (*House Hearings* 1976, pp. 2227–2420), international bankruptcies (*House Hearings* 1976, pp. 1442–56, 1509–17), tax-related issues (*House Hearings* 1976, pp. 2000–34, 2093–2226; *Senate Hearings* 1975, pp. 781–89), transition problems (*House Hearings* 1976, pp. 2621–57), and insurance company bankruptcies and related issues (*House Hearings* 1976, pp. 1582–1619; *Senate Hearings* 1975, pp. 627–63). Such topics, while interesting, were not directly relevant to this study and were therefore not included for consideration.

Once the interest groups and the major organizational issues of reform of the court were ascertained, the Congressional testimony that summarizes this debate was reviewed in its entirety.[2] This testimony was divided into topics of expertise specific to bankruptcy (e.g., dischargeability, exemptions, role of trustees, etc.). But it is the task of the sociologist to stand back from these more narrow, specific, and technical questions in order to analyze and explain the dynamics of a specific event, in this case the event of court reform. These technical categories can inhibit the sociologist's task; but it is an unwritten rule of the social sciences to attempt to penetrate the specialist's language and jargon. (Of course, sociologists themselves are often guilty of then creating their own jargon, an important point to remember but one that cannot be discussed in this context.) For once the sociologist accepts the expert's knowledge as unpenetrable, analysis and explanation are impossible. This is especially true in the fields of law and medicine since these professions have a sizeable investment in keeping the context of their work "secret."

The use of "qualitative" data (i.e., congressional testimony) presents problems of verification and generalization. Yet such data contain a rich and often untapped resource for understanding the tensions of social and organizational change. In this study, the focus on reform emphasizes how and why various groups and organizations approach the possible reform and reorganization of this legal precedure. Alford's (1975) recent study of the health field raises similar methodological problems and also provides useful clues for their solution.

As he asserts, "statements made by individuals are assumed to represent the policy position of the organization they represent and not their personal beliefs" (p. 19). In this study, I have also assumed that the formal testimony of individuals represents the position of their respective groups or organizations. Thus, the testimony was coded to determine the position of various groups on each of the major issues. Quotations were selected for their representativeness of the dominant position of a particular group (e.g. judges, creditors, labor, etc.). After all, as Alford further points out, the "correlation" between individual positions and organizational policy is high since those organizations serve the needs of those individuals.

Table B-2 summarizes, then, the position of interest groups on the issues of reform discussed in chapters 3 to 6. The "x" in the respective cell indicates these positions. Not all groups take a position on all issues of reform. Therefore, a blank in the respective cell indicates that this group's testimony did not include a discussion of that aspect of reform (e.g. representatives of organized labor on the professional or bureaucratic alternative). Also note that some groups take contradictory positions on a particular issue (e.g. credits and bankers on the issue of a redefinition of bankruptcy laws). Of course, a more detailed discussion of these positions can be found in the text.

Table B-2
Critical Issues and Interest Groups of Bankruptcy Court Reform

Interest Groups Political Actors	Bankruptcy Laws: A Redefinition			Organizational Matrix			Organizational Structure			
	Formal/ rational rules	Substantive/ laws	No change	Maintain (local)	Eliminate (cosmopolitan)	No change	Professional alternative	Bureaucratic alternative	Computers[a]	Status quo
Judges		x		x			x			
Lawyers			x	x		x	x			x
Creditors	x	x		x			x	x		x
Bankruptcy Division (A.O.)							x		x	
Legal scholars	x				x			x		
Labor unions	x				x					
Consumer groups			x		x					
U.S. Attorney	x								x	x

Table B-2 — Continued

Interest Groups	Cause of Past Ineffectiveness of Court			Cause of Future Effectiveness of Court			
	Organizational structure	*Open-Credit economy*	*Status quo*	*Educational devices*	*Computers*	*New laws*	*Status quo*
Judges		x					
Lawyers		x			x		
Creditors		x					
Bankruptcy Division (A.O.)							
Legal scholars						x	
Labor unions							
Consumer groups	x			x			
U.S. Attorney							

This is treated as a separate alternative because it emerges as a critical issue in count reform.

Notes

1. See S. 235, the Commission's Bill, and S. 236, the Judges' Bill. These identification numbers refer to the Senate bills; the bills that went before the House are basically the same.

2. The testimony before the House Committee can be found in *Hearings Before the Subcommittee of the Committee on the Judiciary House of Representatives Ninety-Fourth Congress First Session on H.R. 31 and H.R. 32 Bankruptcy Act Revision,* Part I, (Washington, D.C.: Government Printing Office, 1975); *Hearings Before the Subcommittee on the Committee on the Judiciary House of Representatives Ninety-Fourth Congress Second Session on H.R. 31 and H.R. 32,* Part II, III, IV, (Washington, D.C.: Government Printing Office, 1976). The testimony before the Senate Committee can be found in *Hearings Before the Subcommittee on Improvements in Judicial Machinery of the Committee of the Judiciary United States Senate Ninety-Fourth Congress First Session on S. 235 and S. 236,* Part I and Part II (Washington, D.C.: Government Printing Office, 1975).

Appendix C: Factor Analysis for Competitive-Sector Measures in 1960 and 1970

A number of variables describe the political economy of the federal courts, e.g. manufacturing, trade, mining, agriculture, and so on. In 1960 and 1970 the number of available indicators from the census suggests the use of factor scores since the intercorrelation among these measures is strong.

For 1960, the simple correlations presented in table C-1 suggest the development of two indices, one measuring primary industries (mining and agriculture) and another measuring secondary industries (manufacturers, retail-wholesale trade, and value-added). The factor loadings shown in table C-2 confirm this decision. Therefore, in 1960, using factor scores, the competitive sector was measured along these two dimensions.

A similar tack was taken for 1970. The correlations shown in table C-3 suggest three indices: manufacturing, mining, and agriculture; and a factor analysis was used to develop these indices. The resulting factor scores became indicators for this sector of the federal district (table C-4).

This strategy has the advantage of maintaining the "social complexity" (Noell 1974) of the districts at the same time that it reduces the statistical problem of multicollinearity among the independent variables. For a further discussion of the basics of factor analysis, see Childe (1970) and Nie et al. (1975).

Table C-1
Correlation Coefficients (Pearson's r) among the Variables Constituting the Competitive Sector of the U.S. Federal District in 1960

		1	2	3	4	5	6
1. Manufacturing	(1)	—					
2. R-W trade	(2)	.98	—				
3. Value-added	(3)	.57	.51	—			
4. Mining (#)	(4)	.08	.16	.10	—		
5. Mining ($)	(5)	.22	.03	.11	.91	—	
6. Farms (#)	(6)	.59	.50	.11	.52	.48	—

Table C-2

Factor Loadings of the Original Variables on the
Factors of the Competitive Sector in 1960[a]

	Factor 1	Factor 2
Mining (#)	.88	.03
Mining ($)	.98	.05
Farms (#)	.56	.24
Manufacturers	.23	.66
R-W trade	.07	.89
Value-added	.03	.90

[a]Variables analyzed using a varimax rotation. The two
factors account for .786 of the original variance of all six
variables.

Table C-3

Correlation Coefficient (Pearson's r) among the Variables Constituting the
Competitive Sector of the U.S. Federal District in 1970

	1	2	3	4	5	6	7
1. Manufacturing	—						
2. R-W trade	.57	—					
3. Value-added	.82	.80	—				
4. Mining (#)	.19	.06	.04	—			
5. Mining ($)	.33	.32	.24	.69	—		
6. Farms (#)	.24	.27	.06	.57	.53	—	
7. Farms ($)	.40	.20	.26	.20	.22	.53	—

Table C-4

Factor Loadings of the Original Variables on the Factors of the
Competitive Sector in 1970[a]

	Factor 1	Factor 2	Factor 3
Mining (#)	.03	.90	.24
Mining ($)	.02	.87	.06
Farms (#)	−.04	.43	.83
Farms ($)	.06	.01	.72
Manufacturers	.99	.10	.11
R-W trade	.91	.01	.04
Value-added	.92	−.04	−.05

[a]Variables analyzed using a varimax rotation. The three factors account for
.901 of the original variance of all seven variables.

Appendix D: Variable Definitions, Basic Statistics, and Matrices of Simple Correlations for Organizational Data in 1950, 1960, and 1970

This appendix provides the definition of all variables used in this study, basic statistics (mean and standard deviation), and the simple correlation among all variables for each decade.

It should be recalled that all statistics are based upon a sample of eighty-four units that represent the "universe" of all such organizations. Therefore, tests of staistical significance have been omitted. (But for those who are interested, with a total N of eighty-four units correlations are statistically significant at the following levels: $r \geqslant .32$ at the .001 level, $r \geqslant .25$ at the .01 level, and $r \geqslant .18$ at the .05 level.)

Table D-1
Variables Used in Study, with Definitions and Basic Statistics

	Mean	Standard Deviation
1950 Data Set:		
1. *Manufacturing:*[a] all manufacturers with 100 employees plus, all retail and wholesale establishments, all selected services	4.42	.55
2. *Farms:* farms with sales of $40,000 plus	5.66	.65
3. *Median education:* average number of school years completed	8.89	1.11
4. *Median income:* average income	2,365.43	691.33
5. *Population size:*[a] all individuals residing in district	6.21	.71
6. *Population density:*[a] average number of people per square mile per district	2.28	1.11
7. *Pending cases:* all cases not completed by July 1, 1949	396.56	1,145.73

145

Table D–1 – *Continued*

	Mean	*Standard Deviation*
1950 Data Set:		
8. *Filings:* all cases commenced	2,182.86	11,255.72
9. *Demand:* pending and filings	2,579.42	11,358.80
10. *Asset cases:* cases with assets in excess of exempt property	44.89	64.82
11. *Business cases:* Chapter X and XI cases	6.70	11.62
12. *Consumer cases:* Chapter XIII cases	71.49	536.10
13. *Total organizational matrix:* total earnings of lawyers and trustees	14,993.32	24,103.29
14. *Average organizational matrix:* total divided by cases filed	72.41	103.46
15. *Part-time judges:* up to half-time employment	1.31	.85
16. *Full-time judges:* only source of income for these judges	.62	1.04
17. *Terminations:* cases concluded	523.29	1,727.90
18. *Effectiveness:* % paid of creditors' claims	.23	.90
1960 Data Set:[b]		
1. *Merger:* all mergers per district	10.85	22.22
2. *Assets:* median assets of purchasing companies	20.11	28.14
3. *White collar workers:* professional, technical, and kindred workers, and managers and administrators, except farm, and sales, and clerical occupations	5.41	.64
4. *Government employees:*[a] all federal, state, and local government workers	4.42	.37
5. *Median education*	9.32	1.17
6. *Median income*[a]	.39	.21

Table D-1 – *Continued*

	Mean	Standard Deviation
1960 Data Set:[a]		
7. *Savings capital:*[a] savings and investments of the public in savings and loan associations	5.63	.77
8. *Population size*[a]	6.27	.73
9. *Population density*[a]	2.03	.70
10. *Net migration:* population change since 1950, excluding births and deaths	1.38	1.82
11. *Pending cases*	1,000.37	1,696.48
12. *Filings*	1,370.51	2,268.28
13. *Demand*	2,370.88	3,792.32
14. *Asset cases*	124.20	178.72
15. *Business cases*	7.98	16.61
16. *Consumer cases*	161.89	554.79
17. *Organizational matrix*	39,419.29	52,792.30
18. *Average organizational matrix:*	75.00	103.68
19. *Part-time judges*	1.10	1.24
20. *Full-time judges*	1.15	1.81
21. *Terminations*	1,823.62	6,162.17
22. *Effectiveness*	.15	.07
1970 Data Set:		
1. *Mergers*	20.96	43.55
2. *Assets*	40.68	79.19
3. *White collar workers*[a]	5.47	.38
4. *Government employees*[a]	5.26	1.20
5. *Median education*	11.05	1.04
6. *Median income*	4,925.25	998.88

Table D-1 – *Continued*

	Mean	Standard Deviation
1970 Data Set:		
7. *Savings capital*[a]	2.75	.49
8. *Population size*[a]	6.53	1.45
9. *Population density*[a]	2.05	.67
10. *Net migration*[a]	1.18	1.45
11. *Pending cases*	2,168.67	3,389.74
12. *Filings*	2,174.50	3,066.86
13. *Demand*	4,343.16	6,342.84
14. *Asset cases*	264.50	443.25
15. *Business cases*	10.75	21.99
16. *Consumer cases*	333.12	665.71
17. *Organizational matrix*	34,913.02	50,626.22
18. *Average organizational matrix*	15.61	21.13
19. *Part-time judges*	.39	.64
20. *Full-time judges*	2.15	2.25
21. *Clerks:* nonjudicial staff	11.61	13.55
22. *Judicial resources:* salaries of judges	73,592.31	69,348.38
23. *Nonjudicial resources:* salaries of clerks	102,616.44	126,840.06
24. *Terminations*	2,243.89	3,313.54
25. *Effectiveness*	.04	.21

[a]Indicates that respective variable had a skewed distribution and was transformed into logarithmic scale.

[b]Definition of comparable variables are the same in 1950, 1960, and 1970. Therefore, only additional variables for each decade are defined. Table excludes variables based on factor scores; see Appendix C. Also note that all financial figures in 1960 and 1970 of the court's environment have been corrected for inflation using the Consumer Price Index figures and 1950 as a baseline.

Table D-2
Correlation Coefficients (Pearson's r) among All Variables for 1950

	1	2	3	4	5	6	7	8	9	10	11	12	13	14	15	16	17	18
1. Manufacturing	—																	
2. Agriculture	.66	—																
3. Med. education	.03	-.01	—															
4. Med. income	.19	.04	.84	—														
5. Pop. size	.92	.72	-.09	.06	—													
6. Pop. density	.46	-.15	.14	.33	.43	—												
7. Pending	.09	-.08	-.05	—	.07	.13	—											
8. Filings	.41	.40	-.28	-.15	.52	.11	.04	—										
9. Demand	.42	.39	-.28	-.15	.52	.13	.14	.99	—									
10. Asset cases	.35	.04	.30	.47	.21	.42	.27	-.05	-.02	—								
11. Business	.38	.01	.28	.44	.21	.42	.32	-.04	-.01	.85	—							
12. Consumer	-.03	-.10	-.16	-.18	—	-.01	.91	.03	.12	-.01	.08	—						
13. Org'l matrix	.38	—	.11	.25	.23	.42	.22	-.01	.02	.60	.52	.05	—					
14. Average	.06	.12	-.13	-.10	.01	-.13	-.13	-.06	-.07	.03	-.02	-.09	.28	—				
15. Part-time judges	.27	.29	-.11	-.01	.24	.07	.16	.11	.13	.24	.12	.07	.13	.10	—			
16. Full-time judges	.36	-.02	.29	.43	.24	.44	.45	-.05	-.02	.78	.73	.25	.56	-.06	-.11	—		
17. Terms	.04	-.05	-.19	-.05	.03	.06	.30	.77	.79	.13	.13	.20	.14	-.14	.05	.12	—	
18. Effect	—	.12	.08	.02	-.01	-.12	-.04	-.04	-.03	-.03	-.02	-.03	-.01	-.07	-.11	-.02	-.02	—

Table D–3
Correlation Coefficients (Pearson's r) among All Variables for 1960

	1	2	3	4	5	6	7	8	9	10	11	12	13	14	15	16	17	18	19	20	21	22	23	24
1. Merger (#)	—																							
2. Assets ($)	.06	—																						
3. Manufacturing	.60	.11	—																					
4. Mining	−.07	−.03	−.03	—																				
5. # White col.	.33	.02	.67	.19	—																			
6. # Govt. empl.	.50	.05	.78	—	.52	—																		
7. Med. education	.25	.01	.23	−.10	.04	.29	—																	
8. Med. income	.24	.15	.18	−.37	.25	.10	.48	—																
9. Savings cap.	.33	.06	.69	.18	.97	.56	.07	.26	—															
10. Pop. size	.23	—	.57	.21	.98	.39	−.06	.22	.94	—														
11. Pop. density	.51	.07	.65	−.33	.58	.61	.09	.42	.56	.50	—													
12. Net migration	.30	−.08	.39	−.04	.21	.46	.36	.04	.21	.11	.27	—												
13. Pending	.40	—	.41	.06	.21	.43	.13	−.05	.24	.15	.16	.26	—											
14. Filings	.49	.02	.44	.10	.23	.43	.19	.02	.28	.16	.16	.38	.83	—										
15. Demand	.47	.01	.45	.08	.23	.45	.17	−.01	.28	.16	.16	.34	.94	.97	—									
16. Asset cases	.46	.01	.49	.12	.27	.07	.34	.07	.31	.18	.27	.45	.62	.66	.67	—								
17. Business	.81	−.04	.53	−.07	.31	.54	.21	.20	.30	.22	.51	.29	.30	.28	.31	.38	—							
18. Consumer	−.05	−.03	−.01	−.07	−.04	−.01	−.19	−.17	−.05	−.02	−.07	−.15	.62	.27	.44	−.04	−.04	—						
19. Org'l matrix	.63	.03	.61	.09	.35	.67	.28	.07	.39	.25	.34	.52	.70	.78	.79	.81	.50	.50	—					
20. Average	.03	.18	.03	.09	.05	.08	−.20	−.18	.06	.05	.07	.04	−.24	−.27	−.27	−.15	.04	−.18	.03	—				
21. Full-time judges	.54	−.07	.49	.02	.26	.54	.18	.11	.27	.18	.30	.34	.56	.63	.63	.61	.50	.08	.69	−.15	—			
22. Part-time judges	−.03	−.04	−.10	−.02	.08	−.06	−.18	−.07	.02	.11	−.01	−.09	−.07	−.01	−.04	−.11	−.04	−.06	−.09	.04	−.18	—		
23. Terms	.17	—	.04	.13	.01	−.02	.05	−.04	.05	−.02	.04	.21	.25	.52	.42	.18	.07	.08	.21	−.16	.14	−.01	—	

Table D-4
Correlation Coefficients (Pearson's r) among All Variables for 1970

	1	2	3	4	5	6	7	8	9	10	11	12	13	14	15	16	17	18	19	20	21	22	23	24	25	26	27	28
1. Merger (#)	—																											
2. Assets ($)	-.03	—																										
3. Manufacturing	.63		—																									
4. Mining	.11	-.06		—																								
5. Agriculture	.06	-.03			—																							
6. # White col.	.36	-.07	.33	.08	.23	—																						
7. # Govt. empl.	.38	-.06	.37	.60	.29	.28	—																					
8. Med. education	.28	-.03	.27	.07	-.11	.34	.14	—																				
9. Med. income	.47	.04	.55	.02	-.22	.39	.21	.79	—																			
10. Savings cap.	.63	-.06	.61	.30	.19	.40	.74	.29	.42	—																		
11. Pop. size	.37	-.06	.35	.62	.29	.27	.99	.12	.18	.73	—																	
12. Pop. density	.55	.01	.72	-.17	-.13	.20	.31	.19	.60	.41	.28	—																
13. Net migration	.33	-.08	.28	.52	.05	.22	.77	.22	.28	.73	.77	.22	—															
14. Pending	.36	-.04	.39	.28	.23	.25	.66	.16	.20	.71	.64	.20	.57	—														
15. Filings	.41	-.02	.44	.30	.25	.28	.65	.22	.26	.80	.64	.19	.57	.93	—													
16. Demand	.39	-.03	.43	.30	.24	.27	.67	.19	.23	.77	.65	.20	.58	.98	.98	—												
17. Asset cases	.35	-.02	.42	.25	.23	.25	.52	.31	.32	.62	.50	.21	.46	.76	.74	.76	—											
18. Business	.85	-.04	.55	.29	.13	.38	.63	.30	.48	.74	.61	.52	.57	.59	.57	.59	.47	—										
19. Consumer	.09	-.06	.17	.07	.11	.06	.31	-.12	-.09	.30	.30	.03	.23	.76	.63	.71	.33	.24	—									
20. Org'l matrix	.69	-.05	.57	.33	.23	.35	.69	.32	.39	.80	.57	.38	.61	.78	.87	.79	.85	.80	.33	—								
21. Average	.51	-.09	.35	-.09	.06	.10	.09	.03	.13	.13	.08	.36	.04	-.14	-.19	-.17	-.17	.37	-.22	.29	—							
22. Full-time judges	.67	-.04	.69	.29	.21	.38	.65	.29	.44	.87	.65	.45	.57	.82	.87	.86	.75	.75	.49	.87	.11	—						
23. Part-time judges	-.17	-.13	-.24			-.07	-.10	-.10	-.11	-.21	-.10	-.21	-.07	-.10	-.16	-.13	-.09	-.19	.02	-.18	.05	-.27	—					
24. Clerks	.58	-.03	.54	.31	.24	.35	.70	.25	.34	.86	.68	.31	.61	.90	.96	.94	.75	.71	.58	.85	-.02	.93	-.16	—				
25. Salary (Jud)	.66	-.06	.67	.30	.21	.39	.67	.29	.44	.87	.65	.44	.57	.83	.88	.87	.76	.75	.51	.87	.11	.99	-.16	.94	—			
26. Salary (NJ)	.59	-.03	.56	.27	.22	.34	.54	.27	.36	.87	.63	.31	.56	.88	.95	.93	.71	.69	.57	.82	-.04	.92	-.17	.98	.93	—		
27. Terms	.42	-.02	.45	.29	.23	.28	.65	.21	.27	.82	.64	.20	.59	.93	.99	.98	.75	.58	.61	.79	-.17	.87	-.15	.97	.88	.95	—	
28. Effect	-.07	-.06	-.03	-.02	-.17	-.04	-.04	-.13	-.14	-.06	-.03	-.04	-.09	-.08	-.09	-.09	-.07	-.07	-.06	-.08	.08	-.13	.11	-.10	-.12	-.10	-.08	—

Bibliography

"Administration of the Bankruptcy Act." *Report of the Attorney General's Committee on Bankruptcy Administration.* Washington, D.C.: Government Printing Office, 1941.

Aiken, Michael and Jerald Hage. "Organizational Interdependence and Intra-organizational Structure." *American Sociological Review,* 33 (December 1968), 912-30.

Alford, Robert R. *Health Care Politics.* Chicago: University of Chicago Press, 1975.

Anderson, Theodore and Stanley Warkov. "Organizational Size and Functional Complexity: A Study of Administration in Hospitals." *American Sociological Review,* 26 (February 1961), 23-28.

"Announcements of Mergers and Acquisitions." *The National Conference Board.* New York: The National Conference Board, January to December, 1960.

"Announcements of Mergers and Acquisitions." *The National Conference Board,* New York: The National Conference Board, January to December, 1970.

Arnold, Thurman. *The Symbols of Government.* New York: Harcourt, Brace and World, 1962.

Aron, Raymond. "Max Weber and Power Politics." In Otto Stammler (ed.) *Max Weber and Sociology Today.* New York: Harper and Row, 1971, 83-133.

Auerbach, Jerold. *Unequal Justice: Lawyers and Social Change in Modern America.* New York: Oxford University Press, 1976.

Avineri, Shlomo. *The Social and Political Thought of Karl Marx.* London: Cambridge University Press, 1968.

Bachrach, Peter and Morton Baratz. "Two Faces of Power." *American Political Science Review,* 61 (December 1962), 947-52.

Balbus, Isaac. "The Concept of Interest in Pluralist and Marxian Analysis." *Politics and Society,* 1 (February 1971), 151-77.

_____. "The Negation of the Negation: Theory of Capitalism Within an Historical Theory of Social Change." *Politics and Society,* 3 (Fall 1972), 49-63.

_____. *The Dialectics of Legal Repression.* New York: Russell Sage Publications, 1973.

Baran, Paul. "The Concept of the Economic Surplus." In David Horowitz (ed.) *Marx and Modern Economics.* New York: Modern Reader Paperbacks, 1968, 226-51.

Baran, Paul and Paul Sweezy. *Monopoly Capital.* New York: Modern Reader Paperbacks, 1966.

Barett, Edward. "Criminal Justice and the Problem of Mass Production." In Harry Jones (ed.) *The Courts, the Public and the Law Explosion.* Englewood Cliffs, New Jersey: Prentice Hall, 1965.

Barkan, Steven E. "Political Trials and the *'Pro Se'* Defendent in the Adversary System." *Social Problems,* 24 (February 1977), 324–36.

Baker, L. J. "Third Parties and Litigation: A Systematic View of the Judicial Function." *Journal of Politics,* 29 (February 1967), 41–69.

Becker, James. "Class Structure and Conflict in the Managerial Phase: I." *Science and Society,* 37 (Fall 1973), 259–78.

——. "Class Structure and Conflict in the Managerial Phase: II." *Science and Society,* 37 (Winter 1973/1974), 437–54.

Bendix, Reinhard. *Max Weber: An Intellectual Portrait.* New York: Doubleday and Co., 1962.

——. *Work and Authority in Industry.* New York: Harper and Row, 1963.

Bendix, Reinhard and Gunther Roth. *Scholarship and Partisanship: Essays on Max Weber.* Berkeley: University of California Press, 1971.

Benson, J. Kenneth. "Analysis of Bureaucratic-Professional Conflict: Functional versus Dialectical Approaches." *Sociological Quarterly,* 14 (Summer 1973), 376–94.

——. "Organizations: A Dialectical View." *American Sociological Association Annual Meetings.* New York, August, 1973.

Bentley, Arthur F. *The Process of Government.* Chicago: The University of Chicago Press, 1908.

Berman, Jesse. "The Cuban Popular Tribunals." *Columbia Law Review,* 69 (December 1960), 3346–50.

Bernstein, Barton. "New Deal: The Conservative Achievement of Liberal Reform." In Barton Bernstein (ed.) *Towards A New Past: Dissenting Essays in American History.* New York: Vintage Books, 1967, 263–89.

Black, Donald J. "The Mobilization of Law." *The Journal of Legal Studies,* 2 (January 1973), 125–49.

——. *The Behavior of Law.* New York: Academic Press, 1976.

Blalock, Hubert. *Social Statistics.* New York: McGraw-Hill, 1960.

Blau, Peter. *The Dynamics of Bureaucracy.* Chicago: The University of Chicago Press, 1955.

——. "The Hierarchy of Authority in Organizations." *American Journal of Sociology,* 73 (January 1968), 453–67.

——. "Critical Remarks on Weber's Theory of Authority." In Dennis Wrong (ed.) *Max Weber.* Englewood Cliffs, New Jersey: Prentice Hall, 1970a.

——. "A Formal Theory of Differentiation in Organizations." *American Sociological Review,* 35 (April 1970b), 201–218.

Blau, Peter; Wolf Heydebrand, and Robert Stauffer. "The Structure of Small Bureaucracies." *American Sociological Review,* 26 (April 1966), 179–91.

Blau, Peter and Robert Schoenherr. *The Structure of Organizations.* New York: Basic Books, 1971.

Blau, Peter and Richard Scott. *Formal Organizations.* San Francisco: Chandler Publishing Co., 1962.

Blumberg, Abraham. *Criminal Justice.* New York: Quadrangle, 1970.

Boland, Walter. "Size, External Relations and the Distribution of Power: A Study of Colleges and Universities." In Wolf Heydebrand (ed.) *Comparative Organizations: The Results of Empirical Research.* Englewood Cliffs, New Jersey: Prentice-Hall, 1973, 428–41.

Bottomore, Thomas. *Classes in Modern Society.* New York: Basic Books, 1964a.

———. *Elites and Society.* New York: Basic Books, 1964b.

Boulding, Kenneth. "Toward a General Theory of Growth." *The Canadian Journal of Economics and Political Science,* 19 (August 1953), 326–40.

Bowles, Samuel and Herbert Gintis. *Schooling in Capitalist America: Educational Reform and the Contradictions of Economic Life.* New York: Basic Books, 1976.

Braverman, Harry. *Labor and Monopoly Capital.* New York: Monthly Review Press, 1974.

Bredemeier, Harry. "Law as an Integrative Mechanism." In William Evan (ed.) *Law and Society.* New York: The Free Press, 1962, 73–88.

Bronfenbrenner, Martin. *"Das Kapital* for the Modern Man." In David Horowitz (ed.) *Marx and Modern Economics.* New York: Modern Reader Paperbacks, 1968.

Burger, Warren. "Remarks of Warren E. Burger, Chief Justice of the United States, on the State of the Federal Judiciary." In Howard James, *Crisis in the Courts.* New York: David McKay Co., 1971, iii–xii.

———. "Agenda for 2000 A.D.–Need for Systematic Participation." Keynote address at the National Conference on the Causes of Dissatisfaction with the Administration of Justice, St. Paul, Minnesota, 1976.

Caplowitz, David. *Consumers in Trouble.* New York: The Free Press, 1974.

Chamberlain, Neil. "The Corporation and the Trade Union." In E. Mason (ed.) *The Corporation in American Society.* Cambridge, Massachusetts: Harvard University Press, 1966, 122–40.

———. *Enterprise and Environment.* New York: McGraw-Hill, 1968.

Chase, Harold. *Federal Judges: The Appointing Process.* Minneapolis: University of Minnesota Press, 1972.

Childe, Dennis. *The Essentials of Factor Analysis.* New York: Holt, Rinehart and Winston, 1970.

Cicourel, Aaron. *The Social Organization of Juvenile Justice.* New York: John Wiley and Sons, 1968.

Clemente, Frank and Richard Strauss. "The Division of Labor in America: An Ecological Analysis." *Social Forces,* 51 (December 1972), 176–82.

Cohen, Jean. "Max Weber and the Dynamics of Rationalized Domination." *Telos,* 11 (Winter 1972), 63–87.

Commons, J. R. *Legal Foundations of Capitalism.* New York: Macmillan and Co., 1924.

Connolly, William. "The Challenge of Pluralist Theory." In William Connolly (ed.) *The Bias of Pluralism.* New York: Atherton Press, 1964: 3–35.

———. "On 'Interests' in Politics." *Politics and Society,* 2 (Summer 1972): 459–77.

Cook, Beverly. "The Socialization of New Federal Judges: Impact on District Court Business." *Washington University Law Quarterly,* 1971 (Spring 1971), 253–79.

Corwin, Ronald. "Strategies for Organizational Innovation: An Empirical Analysis." *American Sociological Review,* 37 (August 1972), 441–54.

Cyr, Conrad. "Setting the Record Straight for a Comprehensive Revision of the Bankruptcy Act of 1898." *American Bankruptcy Law Journal,* 49 (Spring 1975), 99–171.

Dahrendorf, Ralf. *Class and Class Conflict in Industrial Society.* Stanford: Stanford University Press, 1959.

Davis, Kenneth C. *Administrative Law and Government.* St. Paul, Minnesota: West Publishing Co., 1975.

Dill, William. "Environment as an Influence on Managerial Autonomy." *Administrative Science Quarterly,* 2 (March 1958), 409–443.

Dobb, Maurice. *Political Economy and Capitalism.* London: Routledge, Kegan Paul, 1937.

Dolbeare, Kenneth. *Trial Courts in Urban Politics.* New York: John Wiley and Sons, 1967.

———. "The Federal Courts and Urban Public Policy: An Exploratory Study (1960–1967)." In Joel Grossman and Joseph Tannenhaus (eds.) *Frontiers of Judicial Research.* New York: John Wiley and Sons, 1969, 373–405.

Duncan, Otis et al. *Statistical Geography.* New Yrok: The Free Press, 1961.

Duncan, Otis and Leo F. Schnore. "Cultural, Behavioral and Ecological Perspectives in the Study of Organizations." *American Journal of Sociology,* 65 (September 1959), 132–53.

Durkheim, Emile. *The Division of Labor in Society.* New York: The Free Press: 1964.

Dworkin, Ronald. *Taking Rights Seriously.* Cambridge, Massachusetts: Harvard University Press, 1977.

Edwards, Richard. "Bureaucratic Organization in the Capitalist Firm." In Richard Edwards, Michael Reich, and Thomas E. Weiskoff (eds.) *The Capitalist System: A Radical Analysis of Capitalist American Society.* Englewood Cliffs, New Jersey: Prentice-Hall, 1972.

———. "The Social Relations of Production in the Firm and Labor Market Structure." In Richard Edwards, Michael Reich, and David Gordon (eds.) *Labor Market Segmentation.* Lexington, Massachusetts: D. C. Heath and Company, 1975: 3–27.

Emery, F. E. and E. L. Trist. "The Causal Texture of Organizational Environments." *Human Relations,* 18 (February 1965), 21–31.

Fabricant, Solomon. *The Rising Trend of Government Employment.* New York: National Bureau of Economic Research, Inc., 1949.

Fish, Peter. "Crisis, Politics and Federal Judicial Reform: The Administrative Office Act of 1939." *The Journal of Politics,* 32 (August 1970), 596–627.

———. "Toward a Judicial Administration of Limited Powers: Bankruptcy Crisis and the Administrative Office of the United States Courts." *Journal of the National Conference of Referees in Bankruptcy,* 44 (October 1970), 123–32.

———. *The Politics of Federal Judicial Administration.* Princeton: Princeton University Press, 1973.

Flanders, Stephen. *District Court Studies Project: Interim Report.* Washington, D.C.: Federal Judicial Center, 1976.

Flathman, Richard. *The Public Interest.* New York: John Wiley and Sons, 1966.

Fleming, Machlin. *The Price of Perfect Justice.* New York: Basic Books, 1974.

Frankfurter, Felix and James Landis. *The Business of the Supreme Court: A Study in the Federal Judicial System.* New York: The Macmillan Co., 1927.

Freidson, Eliot. *Profession of Medicine: A Study of the Sociology of Applied Knowledge.* New York: Dodd, Mead, and Co., 1972.

Freund, Julien. *The Sociology of Max Weber.* New York: Pantheon Books, 1968.

Friedman, Lawrence. *The Legal System.* New York: Russell Sage Publications, 1975.

Friendly, Henry. *Federal Jurisdiction: A General View.* New York: Columbia Univerity Press, 1973.

Gallas, Edward; Nesta Gallas; and Ernest Friesen, Jr. *Managing the Courts.* Indianapolis: Bobbs-Merrill Co., 1971.

Garfinkel, Harold. "Conditions of Successful Degradation Ceremonies." *American Journal of Sociology,* 61 (March 1956), 420–24.

Gerth, Hans and C. Wright Mills. *From Max Weber: Essays in Sociology.* New York: Oxford University Press, 1946, 3–70.

Giddens, Anthony. *The Class Structure of the Advanced Societies.* New York: Harper and Row, 1973.

Gintis, Herbert. "The Nature of Labor Exchange and the Theory of Capitalist Production." *The Review of Radical Political Economists,* 8 (Summer 1976), 36–55.

Glaser, William. *Pretrial Discovery and the Adversarial System.* New York: Russell Sage Publications, 1968.

Goldberg, Louis. "Local-Cosmopolitan: Unidimensional or Multidimensional?" *American Journal of Sociology,* 70 (May 1965), 704–710.

Goldman, Sheldon. "Voting Behavior of U.S. Courts of Appeals." *American Political Science Review,* 60 (June 1966), 374–83.

Goldman, Sheldon and Thomas Jahnige. *Federal Courts of a Political System.* New York: Harper and Row, 1971.

Goodwin, R. M. "A Growth Cycle." In C. H. Feinstein (ed.) *Capitalism and*

Economic Growth. Cambridge, England: University of Cambridge Press, 1976, 54–58.

Gordon, David. *Theories of Poverty and Underemployment.* Lexington, Massachusetts: Lexington Books, D.C. Heath and Co., 1972.

Gort, Michael. *Diversification and Integration in American Industry.* Princeton: Princeton University Press, 1962.

Gough, Ian. "Marx's Theory of Productive and Unproductive Labor." *New Left Review,* 76 (November/December 1972) 47–72.

Gouldner, Alvin. *Patterns of Industrial Bureaucracy.* New York: The Free Press, 1954.

_____. "Cosmopolitans and Locals: Toward an Analysis of Latent Social Roles—I." *Administrative Science Quarterly,* 2 (December 1957), 281–306.

_____. "Cosmopolitan and Locals: Toward an Analysis of Latent Social Roles—II." *Administrative Science Quarterly,* 2 (March 1958), 444–80.

_____. *The Coming Crisis of Western Sociology.* New York: Basic Books, 1970.

Grimes, Andrew and Philip Berger. "Cosmopolitan-Local: Evaluation of the Construct." *Administrative Science Quarterly,* 15 (December 1970), 407–417.

Grossman, Joel. "A Model for Judicial Analysis: The Supreme Court and the Sit-In Cases." In Joel Grossman and Joseph Tannenhaus (eds.) *Frontiers of Judicial Research.* New York: John Wiley and Sons, 1969, 405–461.

Grossman, Joel and Austin Sarat. "Litigation in the Federal Courts: A Comparative Perspective." *Law and Society Review,* 9 (Winter 1975), 321–47.

Hage, Jerald and Michael Aiken. *Social Change in Complex Organizations.* New York: Random House, 1970.

Hage, Jerald; Michael Aiken; and Cora Marrett. "Organizational Structures and Communications." *American Sociological Review,* 36 (October 1971), 860–71.

Hall, Richard. "Professionalization and Bureaucratization." *American Sociological Review,* 33 (February 1968), 92–104.

Hamilton, Alexander; James Madison; and John Jay. *The Federalist Papers.* New York: Mentor Books, 1961.

Hannan, Michael and John Freeman. "Growth and Decline Processes in Organizations." *American Sociological Review,* 40 (April 1975), 215–28.

Hartz. Louis. *The Liberal Tradition in America.* New York: Harcourt, Brace and World, 1955.

Hearings Before the Subcommittee on Improvements in Judicial Machinery of the Committee of the Judiciary United States Senate Ninety-Fourth Congress First Session on S. 235 and S. 236, Parts I and II. Washington, D.C.: Government Printing Office, 1975.

Hearings Before the Subcommittee of the Committee on the Judiciary House of Representatives Ninety-Fourth Congress First Session on H.R. 31 and H.R. 32 Bankruptcy Act Revision, Part I. Washington, D.C.: Government Printing Office, 1975.

Hearings Before the Subcommittee of the Committee on the Judiciary House of Representatives Ninety-Fourth Congress First Session on H.R. 31 and H.R. 32 Bankruptcy Act Revision, Parts II, III, IV. Washington, D.C.: Government Printing Office, 1976.

Heilbroner, Robert. *The Limits of American Capitalism.* New York: Harper and Row, 1965.

Hendershot, Gary and Thomas James. "Size and Growth as Determinants of Administrative Production Ratios in Organizations." *American Sociological Review,* 37 (April 1972), 149–53.

Heydebrand, Wolf. "The Study of Organizations." *Social Science Information,* 6 (October 1967), 59–86.

_____. *Hospital Bureaucracy: A Comparative Study of Organizations.* New York: Dunellen Press, 1973a.

_____. "Autonomy Complexity and Non-Bureaucratic Coordination in Professional Organizations." In Wolf Heydebrand (ed.) *Comparative Organizations: The Results of Empirical Research.* Englewood Cliffs, New Jersey: Prentice-Hall, 1973b, 158–89.

_____. "The Technocratic Administration of Justice." Chicago: *American Political Science Association Meetings,* 1976.

_____. "Organizational Contradictions in Public Bureaucracies: Toward a Marxian Theory of Organizations." *Sociological Quarterly,* 18 (Winter 1977a), 83–108.

_____. "Context and Resources of Public Bureaucracies: An Organizational Analysis of Federal District Courts." *Law and Society Review,* 11 (Summer 1977b) pp. 759–821.

Heydebrand, Wolf and James Noell. "Innovation and Task Structure in Professional Organizations." In Wolf Heydebrand (ed.) *Comparative Organizations: The Results of Empirical Research.* Englewood Cliffs, New Jersey: Prentice-Hall, 1973, 294–322.

Heydebrand, Wolf and Carroll Seron. *Adjudication versus Administration: Historical and Political Contradictions of the American Judicial System.* Forthcoming.

Hirsch, Paul. "Organizational Analysis and Industrial Sociology: An Instance of Cultural Lag." *The American Sociologist,* 10 (February 1975), 3–12.

Hogarty, Thomas F. "The Profitability of Corporate Mergers." *Journal of Business,* 43 (July 1970), 317–27.

Holdaway, Edward and Thomas Blowers. "Administrative Ratios and Organizational Size: A Longitudinal Examination." *American Sociological Review,* 36 (April 1971), 278–87.

Horwitz, Morton J. *The Transformation of American Law: 1780–1860.* Cambridge, Massachusetts: Harvard University Press, 1977.

Hurst, James Willard. *The Growth of American Law.* Boston: Little, Brown and Co., 1950.

Jacob, Herbert. *Justice in America.* Boston: Little, Brown and Co., 1965.

———. *Debtors in Court: The Consumption of Government Services.* Chicago: McNally and Co., 1969.

Jacob, Herbert and Kenneth Vines. "The Role of the Judiciary in American State Politics." In Glendon Schubert (ed.) *Judicial Decision Making.* New York: The Free Press, 1963.

Jahnige, Thomas P. and Sheldon Goldman. *The Federal Judicial System.* New York: Holt, Rinehart and Winston, 1968.

Kasarda, John. "The Theory of Ecological Expansion: An Empirical Test." *American Sociological Review,* 40 (December 1975), 165–75.

Katona, George. *The Mass Consumption Society.* New York: McGraw-Hill, 1964.

Kaysen, Carl. "The Corporation: How Much Power?" In Edward Mason (ed.) *The Corporation in Modern Society.* Cambridge, Massachusetts: Harvard University Press, 1966, 85–106.

Kelsen, H. *General Theory of the Law and the State.* Cambridge, Massachusetts: Harvard Univeristy Press, 1945.

Kennedy, Frank. "Restructuring Bankruptcy Administration: The Proposal of the Commission on Bankruptcy Laws." *The Business Lawyer,* 30 (1975), 399–409.

Kennedy, Louanne and Carroll Seron. "Historical and Ecological Analysis of Organizational Formation: The Need for a Combined Approach." San Francisco: *American Sociological Association Annual Meetings,* August 1975.

Kirchheimer, Otto. *Political Justice: The Use of Legal Procedure for Political Ends.* Princeton: Princeton University Press, 1961.

Kolko, Gabriel. *Wealth and Power in America: An Analysis of Social Class and Income Distribution.* New York: Praeger Publishers, 1962.

———. *Triumph of Conservatism.* Chicago: Quadrangle, 1967.

———. *Main Currents in American History.* New York: The Free Press, 1976.

Kriesberg, Louis. "U.S. and U.S.S.R.: Participation in International Non-Governmental Organizations." In Louis Kriesberg (ed.) *Social Processes in International Relations.* New York: John Wiley and Sons, 1968, 466–87.

Latham, Earl. "The Body Politic of Corporations." In Edward Mason (ed.) *The Corporation in Modern Society.* Cambridge, Massachusetts: Harvard University Press, 1966, 218–37.

Lee, Joe. "A Critical Comparison of the Commission Bill and the Judges' Bill for the Amendment of the Bankruptcy Act." *American Bankruptcy Law Journal,* 49 (Winter 1975), 1–49.

Lemert, Edwin. *Social Action and Legal Change: Revolution Within the Juvenile Court.* Chicago: Aldine Publishing Co., 1970.

Leontief, Wassily. "The Significance of Marxian Economics for Present-Day Economic Theory." In David Horowitz (ed.) *Marx and Modern Economics.* New York: Modern Reader Paperbacks, 1968.

Levine, Sol and Paul White. "Exchange as a Conceptual Framework for the Study of Interorganizational Relations." *Administrative Science Quarterly,* 5 (March 1961), 583-601.

Lieberson, Stanley and Irving Allen, Jr. "Location of National Headquarters of Voluntary Associations." *Administrative Science Quarterly,* 8 (December 1963), 316-39.

Lieberson, Stanley and James O'Connor. "Leadership and Organizational Performance: A Study of Large Corporations." *American Sociological Review,* 37 (April 1972), 117-30.

Litwak, Eugene and Lydia Hylton. "Interorganizational Analysis: A Hypothesis on Coordinating Agencies." *Administrative Science Quarterly,* 8 (March 1962), 395-420.

Loewith, Karl. "Weber's Interpretation of the Bourgeois-Capitalistic World in Terms of the Guiding Principle of 'Rationalization.'" In Dennis Wrong (ed.) *Max Weber.* Englewood Cliffs, New Jersey: Prentice-Hall, 1970.

Lowi, Theodore. *The End of Liberalism.* New York: Norton, 1969.

MacKenzie, John. *The Appearance of Justice.* New York: Scribner's and Sons, 1974.

McConnell, Grant. *Private Power and American Democracy.* New York: Alfred A. Knopf and Sons, 1966.

Mannheim, Karl. *Ideology and Utopia.* New York: Harcourt, Brace and World, 1936.

Marcuse, Herbert. "Industrialization and Capitalism." In Otto Stammler (ed.) *Max Weber and Sociology Today.* New York: Harper and Row, 1971, 133-87.

Marglin, Stephen. "What Do Bosses Do? The Origins and Functions of Hierarchy in Capitalist Production, Part I." *Review of Radical Political Economists,* 6 (Summer 1974), 60-112.

_____. "What Do Bosses Do? Part II." *Review of Radical Political Economists,* 7 (Spring 1975), 20-37.

Marrat, Cora. "On the Specification of Interorganizational Dimensions." *Sociology and Social Research,* 56 (October 1971), 83-99.

Marx, Karl. *Capital: A Critique of Political Economy.* New York: International Publishers, 1967.

_____. "Critique of the Philosophy of the State." In Loyd Easton and Kurt H. Guddat (eds.) *Writings of the Young Marx on Philosophy and Society.* New York: Doubledayand Co., 1967, 151-203.

_____. "The Economic and Philosophical Manuscripts of 1844." In Loyd D. Easton and Kurt H. Guddat (eds.) *Writings of the Young Marx on Philosophy and Society.* New York: Doubleday and Co., 1967, 283-338.

_____. *The German Ideology.* New York: International Publishers, 1970.

Mattick, Paul. *Marx and Keynes: The Limits of the Mixed Economy.* Boston: Paul Sargent, 1969.

Means, Gardiner. "Business Concentration in the American Economy." In

Richard Edwards, Michael Reich, and Thomas Weiskoff (eds.) *The Capitalist System: A Radical Analysis of American Society.* Englewood Cliffs, New Jersey: Prentice-Hall, 1972.

Merton, Robert. "Local and Cosmopolitan Influentials." In Roland Warren (ed.) *Perspectives on the American Community: A Book of Readings.* Chicago: Rand McNally and Co., 1966.

Meyer, Marshall. "Some Constraints in Analyzing Data on Organizational Structures: A Comment on Blau's Paper." *American Sociological Review,* 36 (April 1971), 294–97.

––––––. *Bureaucratic Structure and Authority.* New York: Harper and Row, 1972a.

––––––. "Size and the Structure of Organizations: A Causal Analysis." *American Sociological Review,* 37 (August 1972b), 434–40.

––––––. "Organizational Domain." *American Sociological Review,* 40 (October 1975), 599–616.

Mills, C. Wright. *The Power Elite.* New York: Oxford University Press, 1956.

––––––. "The Structure of Power in America." In Irving L. Horowitz (ed.) *Power, Politics, and People.* New York: Ballantine Books, 1963.

––––––. "The Sociology of Stratification." In Irving Horowitz (ed.) *Power, Politics and People.* New York: Ballantine Books, 1963, 305–324.

Montagna, Paul. "Professionalization and Bureaucratization in Large Professional Organizations." *American Journal of Sociology,* 74 (September 1968), 138–45.

Moore, Barrington, Jr. *Origins of Dictatorship and Democracy.* Boston: Beacon Press, 1966.

Mouzelis, Nicos. *Organization and Bureaucracy: An Analysis of Modern Theories.* Chicago: Aldine, Atherton, 1972.

Mueller, Dennis C. "A Theory of Conglomerate Mergers." *Quarterly Journal of Economics,* 83 (November 1969), 643–59.

Murphy, Walter. *Congress and the Court: A Case Study in the American Political Process.* Chicago: University of Chicago Press, 1964.

––––––. *Elements of Judicial Strategy.* Chicago: University of Chicago Press, 1964.

Neghandi, Anant and Bernard Reimann. "Task Environment, Decentralization and Organizational Effectiveness." *Human Relations,* 26 (April 1973), 203–214.

Nicolaus, Martin. "Proletariat and Middle Class in Marx." *Studies on the Left,* 7 (January/February 1967), 22–49.

––––––. "The Unknown Marx." In Robin Blackburn (ed.) *Social Science and Ideology.* New York: Vintage Books, 1973.

Nie, Victor et al. *Statistical Package for the Social Sciences.* New York: McGraw-Hill, 1975.

Noell, James. "On the Administrative Sector of Social Systems: An Analysis of the Size and Complexity of Government Bureaucracies in the American States." *Social Forces,* 52 (June 1974), 549-58.

Nonet, Phillipe. *Administrative Justice: Advocacy and Change in a Government Agency.* New York: Russell Sage Publications, 1969.

O'Connor, James. "Scientific and Ideological Elements in the Economic Theory of Government Policy." *Science and Society,* 33 (Fall/Winter 1969), 385-414.

_____. *The Fiscal Crisis of the State.* New York: St. Martin's Press, 1973.

_____. *The Corporation and the State.* New York: Harper and Row, 1974.

_____. "Productive and Unproductive Labor." *Politics and Society,* 5 (1975): 297-338.

Offe, Claus. "Political Authority and Class Structures—An Analysis of Late Capitalist Societies." *International Journal of Sociology,* 2 (Spring 1972a) 73-108.

_____. "Advanced Capitalism and the Welfare State. *Politics and Society,* 2 (Summer 1972b) 479-88.

Ollman, Bertell. "Marxism and Political Science: Prolegomenon to a Debate on Marx's Method." *Politics and Society,* 3 (Summer 1973), 491-511.

Olson, Mancur. *The Logic of Collective Action: Public Goods and the Theory of Groups.* New York: Schocken, 1971.

Osborn, Richard and James G. Hunt. "Environment and Organizational Effectiveness." *Administrative Science Quarterly,* 19 (June 1974), 231-46.

Parness, Jeffrey. *The Expanding Role of the Parajudge in the United States.* Chicago: American Judicature Society, 1973.

Peltason, Jack. *Federal Courts in the Political Process.* New York: Doubleday and Co., 1955.

Perrow, Charles. "Analysis of Goals in Complex Organizations." *American Sociological Review,* 26 (December 1961), 854-66.

_____. "A Framework for the Comparative Analysis of Organizations." *American Sociological Review,* 32 (April 1967), 194-208.

_____. *Complex Organizations: A Critical Essay.* Glencoe, Illinois: Scott, Foresman and Co., 1972.

Pfeffer, Jeffrey. "Size and Composition of Corporate Boards of Directors: The Organization and Its Environment." *Administrative Science Quarterly,* 17 (June 1972a), 218-28.

_____. "Merger as a Response to Organizational Interdependence." *Administrative Science Quarterly,* 17 (September 1972b), 382-94.

Pfeffer, Jeffrey and Huseyin Leblebici. "Executive Recruitment and the Development of Interfirm Organizations." *Administrative Science Quarterly,* 18 (September 1973a), 449-61.

_____. "The Effect of Competition on Some Dimensions of Organizational

Structure." *Social Forces,* 52 (December 1973b), 268-80.

Piore, Michael. "Notes for a Theory of Labor Market Stratification." In Richard Edwards, Michael Reich, and David Gordon (eds.) *Labor Market Segmentation.* Lexington, Massachusetts: D. C. Heath and Company, 1975: 125-51.

Pivan, Francis Fox and Richard Cloward. *Regulating the Poor: The Functions of Public Welfare.* New York: Random House, 1971.

Polanyi, Karl. "The Role of Markets in Capitalist Society." In Richard Edwards, Michael Reich, and Thomas Weiskoff (eds.) *The Capitalist System: A Radical Analysis of American Society.* Englewood Cliffs, New Jersey: Prentice-Hall, 1972.

Pondy. Louis. "Effects of Size, Complexity and Ownership on Administrative Intensity." *Administrative Science Quarterly,* 14 (March 1969), 47-60.

Price, James. *Handbook of Organizational Measurement.* Lexington, Massachusetts: D. C. Heath and Company, 1972.

Pritchett, Herman. "Division of Opinion Among Justices of the U.S. Supreme Court, 1939-1941." *American Political Science Review,* 35 (October 1941), 890-98.

———. "Public Law and Judicial Behavior." *Journal of Politics,* 30 (May 1968), 480-509.

Pugh, D. C. et al. "Dimensions of Organizational Structure." *Administrative Science Quarterly,* 13 (June 1968), 65-106.

———. "The Context of Organizational Structure." *Administrative Science Quarterly,* 14 (March 1969), 91-114.

Reinstein, Max. "Introduction." In Max Weber *On Law in Economy and Society.* New York: Simon and Schuster, 1954.

Reissman, Leonard. "A Study of Role Conceptions in Bureaucracy." *Social Forces,* 27 (April 1949), 305-310.

Renner, Karl. *The Institutions of Private Law and Their Social Functions.* London: Routledge and Kegan Paul, 1949.

Report of the Commission on Bankruptcy Laws. New York: Commerce Clearing House, 1973.

Richardson, Richard and Kenneth Vines. "Review, Dissent and the Appellate Process: A Political Interpretation." *Journal of Politics,* 29 (August 1967), 597-616.

———. *The Politics of Federal Courts: Lower Courts in the United States.* Boston: Little, Brown and Company, 1970.

Rogin, Michael. "Nonpartisanship and the Group Interest." In Philip Green and Sanford Levinson (eds.) *Power and Community: Dissenting Essays in Political Science.* New York: Vintage Books, 1970.

Rosenberg, Maurice. *The Pretrial Conference and Effective Justice: A Controlled Test in Personal Injury Litigation.* New York: Columbia University Press. 1964.

Roth, Gunther. "Max Weber's Comparative Approach and Historical Typology." In Ivan Vallier (ed.) *Comparative Methods in Sociology.* Berkeley: University of California Press, 1971, 75–97.

Rushing, William. "The Effects of Industry Size and Division of Labor on Administration." *Administrative Science Quarterly,* 12 (September 1967), 273–95.

Schubert, Glendon. *The Public Interest: A Critique of the Theory of a Political Concept.* Glencoe, Illinois: The Free Press, 1960.

_____. *The Political Role of Courts: Judicial Policy Making.* Chicago: Scott, Foresman, and Co., 1965.

_____. *The Judicial Mind: The Attitude and Ideologies of Supreme Court Justices.* Evanston, Illinois: Northwestern University Press, 1965.

Schur, Edwin. *Law and Society: A Sociological View.* New York: Random House, 1968.

Seashore, Stanley and Ephraim Yuchtman. "Factorial Analysis of Organizational Performance." *Administrative Science Quarterly,* 12 (December 1967), 377–96.

Selznick, Philip. *TVA and the Grassroots.* New York: Harper and Row, 1966.

_____. *Law, Society and Industrial Justice.* New York: Russell Sage Publications, 1969.

Seron, Carroll. *Court Reorganization and Judicial Reform.* Ph.D. proposal, New York University, 1973.

_____. "Court Reform: The Rationalization of Legal Organizations." Unpublished. Yale University, 1976.

Shuchman, Philip. "The Fraud Exemption in Consumer Bankruptcy." *Stanford Law Review,* 23 (April 1971), 735–73.

_____. "An Attempt at a 'Philosophy' of Bankruptcy." *UCLA Law Review,* 21 (1973/1974), 403–476.

Simpson, Richard and William Gulley. "Goals, Environmental Pressures and Organizational Characteristics." *American Sociological Review,* 27 (June 1962), 344–51.

Skolnick, Jerome: *Justice Without Trial: Law Enforcement in a Democratic Society.* New York: John Wiley and Sons, 1966.

Smigel, Erwin. *The Wall Street Lawyer: The Professional Man.* New York: The Free Press, 1964.

Stammler, Otto. (ed.) *Max Weber and Sociology Today.* New York: Harper and Row, 1971.

Stanley, David et al. *Bankruptcy: Problem, Process, Reform.* Washington, D.C.: Brookings Institution, 1971.

Stinchcombe, Arthur. "Bureaucratic and Craft Administration of Production: A Comparative Study." *Administrative Science Quarterly,* 4 (September 1959), 168–87.

_____. "Social Structure and Organizations." In James March (ed.) *Handbook of Organizations*. Chicago: McNally and Co., 1965.

Tables of Bankruptcy Statistics with Reference to Bankruptcy Cases Commenced and Terminated in the United States District Courts During the Fiscal Year Ending June 30, 1950. Washington, D.C.: Government Printing Office, 1950.

Tables on Bankruptcy Statistics With Reference to Bankruptcy Cases Commenced and Terminated in the United States District Courts During the Fiscal Year Ending June 30, 1960. Washington, D.C.: Government Printing Office, 1960.

Tables on Bankruptcy Statistics with Reference to Bankruptcy Cases Commenced and Terminated in the United States District Court During the Fiscal Year Ending June 30, 1969. Washington, D.C.: Government Printing Office, 1969.

Terreberry, Shirley. "The Evolution of Organizational Environments." *Administrative Science Quarterly,* 13 (March 1968), 590–613.

Thompson, Edward P. *The Making of the English Working Class*. New York: Pantheon Books, 1964.

Thompson, James D. *Organizations in Action*. New York: McGraw-Hill, 1967.

Thompson, James D. and William McEwen. "Organizational Goals and Environment." *American Sociological Review,* 23 (February 1958), 23–31.

Trubeck, David M. "Max Weber on Law and the Rise of Capitalism." *Wisconsin Law Review,* 1972 (1972): 720–54.

Truman, David. *The Governmental Process: Political Interests and Public Opinions.* New York: Alfred A. Knopf, 1951.

Udy, Stanley. "The Comparative Analysis of Organizations." In James March (ed.) *Handbook of Organizations*. Chicago: McNally and Co., 1965.

Unger, Roberto Mangabeira. *Law in Modern Society: Toward a Criticism of Social Theory*. New York: The Free Press, 1976.

United States Budget in Brief. Washington, D.C.: Government Printing Office, 1952.

United States Budget in Brief. Washington, D.C., Government Printing Office, 1962.

United States Budget in Brief. Washington, D.C., Government Printing Office, 1972.

U.S. Bureau of the Census. *City and County Data Books*. Washington, D.C.: Government Printing Office, 1952.

_____. *City and County Data Books*. Washington, D.C.: Government Printing Office, 1962.

_____. *City and County Data Books*. Washington, D.C.: Government Printing Office, 1972.

United States Code Annotated, Title 28, St. Paul, Minnesota: West Publishing Co., 1969.

United States Code, Title II, Sections 68 and 102. Washington, D.C., Government Printing Office, 1971.

Vines, Kenneth. "Federal District Judges and Race Relations Cases in the South." *Journal of Politics,* 26 (May 1964), 337–57.

———. "The Role of the Circuit Courts of Appeals in the Federal Judicial Process." In Walter Murphy (ed.) *Courts, Judges and Politics.* New York: Random House, 1974.

Vukowich, William. "Debtors' Exemptions Rights." *Georgetown Law Review,* 62 (February 1974), 779–878.

Warren, Charles. *The Supreme Court in United States History.* Boston: Little, Brown and Co., 1926.

Warren, Roland. "Toward a Typology of Extra-Community Controls Limiting Local Community Autonomy." *Social Forces,* 34 (May 1956), 338–41.

———. "The Interorganizational Field as a Focus for Investigation." *Administrative Science Quarterly,* 12 (December 1967a), 396–400.

———. "Interaction of Community Decision Organizations: Some Basic Concepts and Needed Research." *Social Service Review,* 41 (September 1967b), 261–70.

Weber, Max. *On Law in Economy and Society.* New York: Simon and Schuster, 1954.

———. "Bureaucracy." In Hans Gerth and C. Wright Mills (eds.) *From Max Weber: Essays in Sociology.* New York: Oxford University Press, 1946a, 196–266.

———. "Class, Status and Party." In Hans Gerth and C. Wright Mills (eds.) *From Max Weber: Essays in Sociology.* New York: Oxford University Press, 1946b.

———. "Politics as a Vocation." In Hans Gerth and C. Wright Mills (eds.) *From Max Weber: Essays in Sociology.* New York: Oxford University Press, 1946c.

———. *General Economic History.* New York: The Free Press, 1956.

———. *The Protestant Ethic and the Spirit of Capitalism.* New York: Scribner and Sons, 1958.

———. "Routinization of Charisma." In Talcott Parsons (ed.) *Structure and Process in Modern Organizations.* New York: The Free Press, 1960.

———. "Types of Authority and Imperative Coordination." In Talcott Parsons (ed.) *The Theory of Social and Economic Organization.* New York: The Free Press, 1964.

———. *Economy and Society, Volume I.* New York: Bedminster Press, 1968, 212–302.

Weinstein, James. *The Corporate Ideal and the Liberal State.* Boston: Beacon Press, 1968.

Weston, J. Fred. *The Role of Mergers in the Growth of Large Firms.* Berkeley: University of California Press, 1953.

Williams, William A. *The Contours of American History*. Cleveland: World Publishing Co., 1961.

Wirth, Louis. "Urbanism as a Way of Life." In Richard Sennett (ed.) *Classic Essays on the Culture of the City*. New York: Appleton-Century-Crofts, 1969, 143–64.

Wolfe, Alan. "Political Repression and the Liberal Democratic State." *Monthly Review*, 23 (December 1971), 18–39.

_____. *The Seamy Side of Democracy*. New York: David McKay Co., 1973.

Wolff, Robert Paul. *The Poverty of Liberalism*. Boston: Beacon Press, 1968.

Wolin, Sheldon. *Politics and Vision: Continuity and Innovation in Western Political Thought*. Boston: Little, Brown and Co., 1960.

Wright, Erik. "To Control or to Smash Bureaucracy: Weber and Lenin on Politics, the State and Bureaucracy." *Berkeley Journal of Sociology*, 21 (1974), 69–108.

Zald, Meyer. "The Power and Functions of Boards of Directors: A Theoretical Synthesis." *American Journal of Sociology*, 75 (July 1969), 97–111.

_____ . *Organizational Change: The Political Economy of the YMCA*. Chicago: University of Chicago Press, 1970.

Zeisal, Hans et al. *Delay in the Courts*. Boston: Little, Brown and Co., 1959.

Index

Index

Adjudication, rationalization of, 55–57

Alford, Robert R., 19. 126

Allocations from Congress, resources derived from, 82–83

American Bar Association (ABA), 52–53

Anderson, Theodore, 85

Asset cases, 34, 84; effect of environmental variables on, 45, 46

Attorneys, practicing, 125; on causes of Bankruptcy Court's ineffectiveness, 117; on future role of Bankruptcy Court, 119–20; position of, on bankruptcy reform, 73–74, 104–105; role of, in court's organizational matrix, 63–66; their view of court's task structure, 51, 53, 55

Attorney's Office, U.S.: position of, on bankruptcy reform, 98–99; their view of court's task structure, 51, 55

Auerbach, Jerold, 2, 3, 36, 65, 67, 78

Bachrach, Peter, 19

Balbus, Isaac, 19, 20, 130

Bankers: position of, on bankruptcy reform, 104; their view of court's task structure, 50–51

Bankruptcy Act (1938), 16

Bankruptcy cases: consumer, 33, 34; corporate or business, 33–34; effect of environmental variables on asset, business, and consumer, 45–48; effect of environmental variables on pending, 42, 44; number and complexity of, 31–34; post-WWII increase in, 1; proposals for reform of, 1–3

Bankruptcy Code, 2, 4, 15, 53; Chapter VII of, 52; Chapters X and XI of, 34, 51–52; Chapter XIII of, 33, 34, 47–48, 75

Bankruptcy Court, United States, 1–3; analysis of, as established by 1938 legislative mandate, 15–18; caseload of (1950 to 1970), 42–45; caseload and casemix of (1930 to 1970), 31–34; casemix of (1950 to 1970), 45–48; causes of ineffectiveness in, 117–118; environment of, 34–42; establishment date of, 13, 14; future role of, 118–121; organizational effectiveness of (1950 to 1970), 114–116; organizational matrix of (1950 to 1970), 63–66; organizational matrix and size of, 92; overview of, 3–7; personnel and resources of (1950 to 1970), 5, 16–17, 23, 82–85; politics of caseload and casemix of, 48–55; reform of, 18–24, 121–122, 125–131; research strategy for studying, 14–15; size of, 5, 16–17, 23; task environment, personnel, and resources of, 85–95; task structure, organizational matrix, and size of (1950 to 1970), 94–95; task structure and size of, 91–92. *See also* Commission's Bill; Judges' Bill

Bankruptcy Division (of Administrative Office of United States Court), 97, 105; position of, on bankruptcy reform, 102–103

Baran, Paul, 40, 45, 47

Baratz, Morton, 19

Bendix, Reinhard, 9, 19, 21, 102, 110

Bentley, Arthur F., 19

Black, Donald J., 66

Blau, Peter, 7, 9, 11, 47, 85

Blumberg, Abraham, 81, 95

Boland, Walter, 85

Bottomore, Thomas, 39

Bowles, Samuel, 41, 45

171

About the Author

Carroll Seron is an assistant professor of sociology and political economy at the University of Texas at Dallas. She received the B.A. from the University of California at Santa Cruz, the Ph.D. from New York University, and did post-doctoral work in law at Yale University. She is also the coauthor with Wolf Heydebrand of a forthcoming book entitled *Adjudication versus Administration: Historical and Political Contradictions of the American Judicial System.*